ANNIE MAHLE

SUGAR
& SALT

A YEAR AT HOME
AND AT SEA

Sugar & Salt: A Year At Home and At Sea
Book One - The Blue Book

Some recipes included in this book were previously published in the *Portland Press Herald*.

Printed in the United States of America by Kirkwood Printing, Wilmington, MA
Printed locally, on recycled paper, because we believe in sustainable interactions with our neighbors and our earth.

Book design by MORE & Co. – Maria Alexandra Vettese, Christopher David Ryan and Ryan Thomas Shimala, Portland, ME
Development editing by Dana Degenhardt
Copyediting by David Osterman and Norma Mahle

ISBN: 978-0-9749706-1-5
Library of Congress Control Number: 2012910645

Baggywrinkle Publishing
136 Holmes St.
Rockland, ME 04841
1-800-869-0604
www.athomeatsea.com
www.mainewindjammer.com

For my family...
Every day with you is
rich and blessed.

Contents

Introduction

My life is lived in two distinct places, I cook in both, but the settings of each are very different. When I'm at home in the winter, my meals are about family and the occasional entertaining meal with friends and extended family. When I'm at sea, I'm cooking for 30 people every day on my floating, sailing restaurant, the Schooner *J. & E. Riggin*. Unusual, perhaps, but not as unfamiliar as might seem at first glance, as food and community are what bring us all together and that happens on a daily basis whether at our small family table or around a larger table with a larger family of guests who sail with us during the summer months.

Whether the table is small or large, the importance of gathering to pause, give thanks, eat well and laugh together is not to be underestimated, no matter how mundane or routine. Those moments become snapshots. Individual moments, like the grains of sand on a beach; each moment, when gathered together, creating the whole. I feel the same about the food I use and the meals I create from them. Each of the ingredients, plus the thought, the time, even the presentation are all individual parts that become the whole.

This book and my life contain both sugar and salt; which is no surprise as they are basic ingredients in cooking. But my salt isn't only the salt at the table or on the counter; it's the salty ocean that surrounds my family, my work, and my food as I cook for my passengers/guests each year, from May through October, as we sail our way past the islands of Penobscot Bay, Maine. The food that I create there, and just as carefully (though in much smaller quantities!) at home for my family in the winter, all becomes a part of the individual, indivisible, moments of my life.

I suppose it's no surprise that it's the simplest things – for both food and memories – that stand out. I've often found that the simplest meals are the ones that are remembered most. I think that may be part of the reason that many of our passengers return year after year; the memories created on the *Riggin* are, while simple, nearly impossible to forget.

In this book, and future books in this series, I want to share bits of my life – not just recipes, but the choices and thoughts behind the recipes. Because I'm constantly creating, this cookbook is one of many that will become a series, not just one that will stand alone. It's written with flexibility and seasonality woven throughout its pages. Most specifically the Leftover pieces (pages 22, 110 and 120) and Creative Kitchen (page 88) give you a window into how I think about the creation of my meals. Organized by month, the recipes have enough structure for someone shopping at the grocery store and enough detail for those picking straight from the garden.

Then and Now

My love affair with Maine, sailing, food and the blue-eyed, bearded man in my life all began the same summer. Before that, Maine was that place between Canada and the Atlantic Ocean, I didn't know what a schooner was, food came exclusively from the grocery store, and the blue-eyed man was a blue-eyed dream.

In the last stages of my senior year at Michigan State University I knew that I wanted to learn how to sail, I wanted to travel, and I *didn't* want to call home for money. Enter serendipity and some good universal juju juice and… I met a friend who knew someone… whose parents owned a boat in Maine… and these parents were looking for a mess cook who could start immediately. I was so excited to get the job that when my mom asked how much it paid, I didn't have an answer for her; I never asked!

Two days (and nearly 24 hours of tag-team driving) after graduating from college, I was in Maine, on a schooner. That morning, I met Jon, the blue-eyed, bearded man; he's now my husband, Captain Jon Finger. He's also known as Papa to our two daughters, Chlöe and Ella. And since 1998, we've owned, sailed, and cherished the Maine windjammer, the Schooner *J. & E. Riggin*.

On schooners, I found a seemingly never ending curiosity about food made by hand. Yeasty dough rising on the warming shelf by the stove pipe, jams made from strawberries picked and delivered the same day and New England Boiled Dinner made from brisket corned by the local butcher. Everything tasted so good and had such integrity of place.

As I've worked my way up from mess cook to Chef/Owner, my journey has mirrored the food movement in this country. Finding that food doesn't just show up on grocery store shelves. Discovering that the best food often comes from ingredients straight from the local farm, the local butcher, and/or my garden. Learning, sharing and exploring food made by hand.

After working for other boats and restaurants for years and finding ourselves far away from home, pregnant with our first of two and needing a change, we decided to come

back to Maine, the home of our hearts and become windjammer owners. So began our adventurous, hilarious, sometimes frenetic, unique life together as business owners and stewards of the Schooner *J. & E. Riggin*. While technically we bought a boat and a business, in truth we entered a lifestyle and a way of living – seasonal, satisfying, challenging and adventurous.

Land and Sea

The *Riggin* is as much a restaurant and inn as she is a two-masted sailing schooner. She is a National Historic Landmark, with her own place in American history. Built in 1927 on the Maurice River in Dorchester, New Jersey as an oyster dredger, her varied past always included some sort of fishing until the 1970's. By then motors had completely replaced sail as a method of commercial fishing and transportation so the *Riggin* was converted to a passenger-carrying vessel; she's one of the very few, very lucky survivors of the Age of Sail.

Now, nearly 85 years after she was first launched, Jon, our crew, the *Riggin* and I welcome up to 24 guests, from all walks of life and all parts of the world, who will spend between 4 and 10 days sailing in and around one of the most magical sailing grounds in the world, Penobscot Bay. Sometimes the guest list is a collection of single travelers, couples, friends and families who don't know each other before the trip begins, but who are closely bonded by the end in the same way childhood relationships form at summer sleepover camp. Sometimes a school, crafting group or a family charters the *Riggin* and they have the entire boat for themselves.

In all cases, Penobscot Bay, Maine offers its pine-studded, granite strewn shores and its deep mossy-green waters which bodly wrap around and take hold in the most elemental of ways. Each trip on the *Riggin* is an authentic and unique experience, using wind and tide to wend our way among islands that were created centuries ago and will solidly remain for centuries after we pass.

And as we sail, I cook. While a captain's license is also a part of my resume, standing in front of my wood stove creating is what I really love.

Sugar and Salt

The focus of my food, both for my family in the winter and our guests and crew in the summer, is the same; I want it to be sustainable, and, whenever possible, local. Where the food comes from, who grows or makes it, how it's produced – all of this impacts the final product. Starting with fresh ingredients, I can focus on flavorful, comforting, and approachable meals. It's classic, crafted, and intentional because ingredients matter. While not everything my guests and family eat is organic, local or handmade, it's a significant focus in my cooking. The balance of time vs. quality is one that I walk, just like everyone else, meal to meal.

Where I cook matters less to me than that I DO cook. That I cook on a wood stove, essentially outside, without electricity, with minimal water and refrigeration for 30 people every day of the summer only means my recipes are time-tested and uncomplicated. It's not expected that anyone would want to duplicate those conditions - some days even I don't. However, if I can make meals taste good under those conditions, anyone can make these recipes in a home kitchen.

I am constantly adapting favorite recipes to accommodate a newly foraged ingredient, so my recipes are always developing, changing and evolving, while staying true to the intent; comfort, flavor, and family. I hope you find that *Sugar and Salt* is more than a collection of recipes and thoughts; I hope it becomes a springboard for your own creativity.

Happy hearts and fully bellies,
Annie
May 2012
Lat 44N 5' 47.93" Long 69W 7' 1.47"
Rockland, Maine

January

For me cooking food is sometimes as much
about making memories as it is about
nourishment. Like the moment one of my
girls comes in from a cold, white, snow-
covered romp in the snow. Snowflake
crystals glinting off her coat, Ella is slowly
freed from her cumbersome snow pants,
jacket and scarf; these, plus her soggy mit-
tens, are hung to dry. Moving freely now,
she makes her way into the kitchen, where
a simmering pot of soup emits steam that
fogs the windows. She sits down to a warm
bowl with oyster crackers floating on the
surface.

Chicken and White Bean Chili

Serves 6 to 8

2 cups dry cannellini beans
2 tablespoons olive oil
1 1/2 to 2 pounds boneless chicken thighs cut into 1-inch pieces
1/2 teaspoon ground cayenne
1 1/2 tablespoons chili powder
1 1/2 tablespoons ground cumin
1 tablespoon kosher salt
1 cup peeled and diced carrots; about 1 large carrot
1 cup thinly sliced scallions; about 4 or 5 scallions
1/2 yellow bell pepper, cored, seeded and diced; about 1 cup
2 tablespoons minced garlic; about 6 cloves
6 cups chicken broth
water if needed

Garnish (optional)
Yogurt and Chive Sauce (see below)
1/2 cup sour cream
2 ounces grated Cheddar cheese; about 1 cup lightly packed
1 cup thinly sliced scallions; about 4 or 5 scallions

Place the beans in a large pot or bowl and cover with water for at least two hours or over-night. Heat a medium-sized stockpot over medium-high heat. Heat the oil and add the chicken thighs, spices and salt. Sauté for 5 minutes or until the chicken begins to brown. Add the vegetables and garlic and sauté for another 8 to 10 minutes. When the mixture begins to stick to the bottom and most of the moisture has evaporated, add the white beans and chicken broth. Bring to a boil, reduce to a simmer and simmer for 1 1/2 hours or until the beans are tender. You may need to add more water or broth during cooking. Garnish with your choice of Yogurt and Chive Sauce, sour cream, grated cheddar cheese and/or diced green onion.

Yogurt and Chive Sauce

Makes 1 1/4 cups

1 cup plain yogurt
1 tablespoon minced chives
1/4 cup diced tomatoes
1/4 teaspoon salt

1 teaspoon lime juice; less than 1/2 a lime
pinch cayenne pepper

Mix all ingredients together and serve with the chili.

Cauliflower, Cheddar and Jalapeno Soup

This soup is great with ale or another full-flavored beer. Serves 4 to 6

2 tablespoons vegetable oil
2 cups diced onions; about 1 large onion
3 tablespoons minced jalapeno pepper, cored and seeded (for more heat retain the seeds);
about 1/2 a large jalapeno pepper
2 teaspoons kosher salt
1/4 teaspoon freshly ground black pepper
2 tablespoons minced garlic; about 6 cloves
6 cups cauliflower, chopped coarsely; about one head using the most of the white stem
3 tablespoons all-purpose flour
4 cups low-salt chicken broth
2 cups milk
4 ounces grated Cheddar cheese; about 2 cups lightly packed

Heat a medium-sized stockpot over medium-high heat; add the oil then the onions, jalapeno, salt and pepper and sauté until the onions are translucent, about 10 minutes. Add
the garlic and cauliflower and sauté for another 10 minutes or until tender. Add the flour
and stir until completely incorporated and then add the broth, stirring vigorously until the
flour is dissolved. Bring to a simmer and cook for 20 minutes. Remove from heat, add the
milk and Cheddar cheese and stir until fully melted. Do not bring the heat up high once
the cheese has been added. Serve as is, or puree the soup until it is smooth. To reheat,
allow time for the soup to come to temperature over low to medium heat. This will insure
that the soup doesn't break. Serve with salad and crusty bread.

Cream of Mushroom Soup – Asian Style

Serves 4 to 6

1 pound fresh shitake mushrooms, de-stemmed and sliced (stems reserved)
2 1/2 cups water
2 tablespoons unsalted butter
2 cups diced onions; about 2 medium onions (peels and stems reserved)
1 tablespoon minced garlic; about 3 cloves

2 cups scallions, cut into 1-inch pieces; about 2 bunches (ends reserved)
1 teaspoon kosher salt
1/8 teaspoon freshly ground black pepper
1 teaspoon ground allspice
1/2 teaspoon ground cloves
4 cups low-salt vegetable or chicken broth
2 teaspoons tamari or soy sauce
1 cup heavy cream

Save the shitake mushroom stems, the ends of the scallions and the onion peels and add to a small stockpot with the water. Bring to a boil and then reduce to a simmer. In a medium stockpot, melt butter and add the Vidalia onions. Sauté onions until they are translucent, about 10 minutes. Add the shitake mushrooms, garlic, salt, pepper and spices and sauté another 5 minutes. Strain and reserve the simmering liquid; add vegetable broth to make 6 cups. Add the broth and tamari to the onions and mushrooms. Simmer for 30 minutes. Add the cream and scallions and simmer for another 5 minutes.

For a more finished look, reserve the scallions, uncooked, and serve them as a garnish.

Spicy Handkerchief Pasta and Sausage Soup

Crushing seeds is easily done by a few pulses in a spice grinder. Alternately, you can crush fennel seeds by using the bottom of a skillet to press them on a cutting board. Serves 4 to 6 generously

2 tablespoons olive oil
1 pound sweet Italian sausage, casing removed
4 cups minced fennel bulb; about 1 large bulb
2 cups minced onion; about 1 large onion
2 teaspoons kosher salt
1 tablespoon fennel seeds, crushed
1/8 teaspoon red pepper flakes (optional)
1 1/2 tablespoons minced fresh rosemary; about 1 large (5-inch) sprig
1 cup white wine
8 cups low-salt chicken broth
1/4 cup minced fresh parsley
1 Pasta recipe (page 17) or 2 cups dried pasta of your choice

Heat a large stockpot over medium-high heat. Add the olive oil and the sausage and sauté until it begins to brown, using a wooden spoon to break it up occasionally. While the sausage is browning, make the pasta dough. Add the fennel, onion, salt, fennel seeds, red pepper flakes and rosemary. Sauté until the fennel and onions are soft and translucent, about 10 minutes. Add the white wine and reduce by half. Add the chicken broth and bring to a boil. Reduce to a simmer and roll out the pasta. Add the parsley and pasta; stir and cook until the pasta squares rise to the surface.

Handkerchief Pasta

Makes 2 servings or enough for Spicy Handkerchief Pasta and Sausage Soup (page 16)

1 cup all-purpose flour
1 egg
4 tablespoons (or so) of water
2 pinches of salt

With either a dough hook or by hand, mix all of the ingredients together, adding the water 1 tablespoon at a time as needed. Knead for 5 minutes with a dough hook or 10 minutes by hand. Cover with plastic wrap and let rest while you make the remainder of the soup. After you add the chicken broth to the soup, roll out the pasta dough to 1/8-inch thick and use either a pizza cutter, pastry roller or a knife to cut it into 1-inch squares. Add to the stockpot when the soup has come to a boil.

BY HAND
Handsewn Apron

The tools of a cook's trade take many shapes and forms – knives, cutting boards, whisks and strainers –and are influenced by ethnicity, geography and place (restaurant kitchen vs. campfire.) One tool that is constant throughout, but also takes many forms, is a cook's apron.

My grandmother used to have at least one hanging in the pantry always ready for use. They were the bibbed kind made with cotton gingham and decorated with ruffles around the edges. My dad, the dishwasher and general after-dinner manager, often wears one to protect his clothes; they range from my grandma's old ruffled ones to a basic dish towel tucked into the waistband of his pants. My mom, especially on holidays, wears one. Our girls have outgrown the ones that I made of oil cloth which are water proof and perfect for finger painting and other messy projects. I wear one constantly. In years past it was the traditional white chef's apron but now that my galley is less formal, my aprons have more personality.

The apron I reach for depends on my mood and the task at hand. Many of mine are homemade, some are old, and a number of them use recycled material. No matter what, however, part of my everyday routine before I begin cooking is to choose an apron that suits my day.

Because I use aprons every day, and have mess cooks/assistants who also need to be kept well stocked with aprons, I make a lot of my own. Because I need comfortable, easy to wash aprons, and because I love anything upcycled, I often make them from t-shirts.

When I begin my search for suitable fabrics for the apron projects that swim around in my head, my thoughts turn, not to a fabric store, but either to our barn (the repository for all old, ill-fitting, under-loved clothing) or to Goodwill. Of course one could purchase a brand new cotton-jersey t-shirt for this project or buy cotton-jersey off a bolt, but chances are the quality won't be what is needed with the former (regular undershirt material is too thin,) and the latter can be difficult to find. I've had much better luck prowling second hand shops. Not to mention, the hunt is so much fun.

Feel the weight of the fabric - for an apron, the heavier the better. Avoid the popular lighter-weight fabrics or the less well-made which will pill when washed and just aren't up to the task for this project. When selecting a t-shirt, don't fret if the tees you find have pockets, logos or stains. All can either be removed or incorporated into your project.

The idea for this apron comes from one of my favorite clothing designers, Natalie Chanin. Her work consistently incorporates recycled fabric, creating new pieces from old, unloved clothing or fabric. Much of her clothing is handsewn in the US by seamstresses who bid on the work. One foundation of her style is not only to show the stitches, but to highlight them rather than hide them, making them an integral part of the beauty of her designs. She often allows the raw edges of the fabric to show and with cotton they curl a little, but don't fray, which also becomes part of the beauty and simplicity of her designs.

Supplies
One white cotton-jersey t-shirt that is at least 23-inches wide
One colored cotton-jersey t-shirt
Garment scissors (or rotary cutter, self-healing cutting mat and ruler)
Pins
Button and carpet thread (a very strong thread found at well stocked fabric stores or online) in either a matching or contrasting color
Sharp needle, #9 (or one of your choosing)

1. Lay the white t-shirt out flat on a work table or over a self-healing cutting mat. With a pair of garment scissors or a rotary cutter and ruler, make a horizontal cut through both layers of the shirt just under the arm pits of the t-shirt from arm pit to arm pit. You can choose to remove the bottom hem if you wish. I usually leave it as a design element. Cut the arms off the t-shirt and then cut 2 long, 2-inch wide strips from the bib of the t-shirt. These will become the apron ties.

2. You now have a tube with open ends at the top and bottom. Vertically cut through the tube on each side, creating two separate rectangles making sure to remove the side seams if present. This is the skirt of your apron.

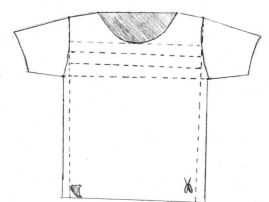

3. Lay the colored t-shirt flat on your work surface and cut a 2-inch wide strip from the bottom (discard the hem), which is 1 1/4-inches shorter than the width of the apron.

4. Place the two large rectangles (the apron skirt) on your work surface, one on top of the other, and pin the edges every 5 inches or so around all four sides.

5. Double thread the needle and knot the thread. Sew the two pieces together on all four sides using a running stitch, knots on the top surface, leaving a 1/4-inch seam allowance. The thread and knots should be visible as a design element on the surface of your work.

6. Lay the two sewn rectangles flat again and lay the colored strip of fabric across the bottom edge leaving 5/8-inches on either side and 1 1/4-inch at the bottom.

7. Pin the color strip every 5 inches or so and sew with a running stitch on all four sides leaving a 1/4-inch seam allowance.

8. Fold the ties in third, pin the ties on the backside of the top two corners and sew in an x pattern.

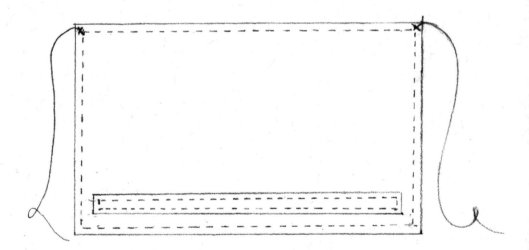

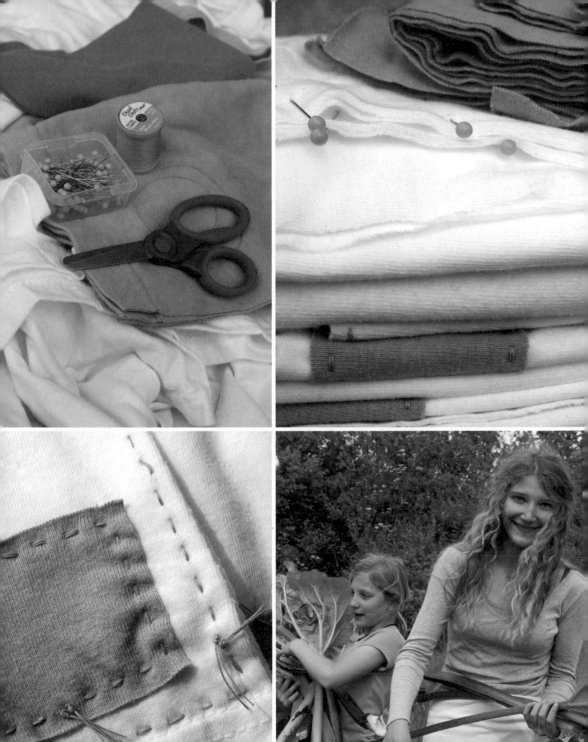

LEFTOVERS DONE RIGHT
Comfort in a Bowl

As the fall winds push their way down from the north, bringing crisp blue skies, wind-chapped cheeks and exhilarating sailing, my soup pot comes out and I begin serving up ladle after ladle of hand-warming, belly-satisfying soup.

The beauty of soup is that it's perfect for using up little bits of this 'n' that which are not enough to make a meal, but are full of flavor. There is almost nothing that can't be made into a warm, rich soup with the addition of well-sautéed onions, garlic, and some chicken or vegetable broth. If you are not a vegetarian, then the addition of bacon or pancetta is a sure flavor boost as well.

Here are some suggestions for getting the most out of what you have to get every bit of flavor out of the fridge, and into a meal. Bones from a whole roast chicken, roast beef, or ham can be simmered in water with onions, carrots and celery for an impromptu broth. It won't be as fully-flavored as true stock, but its leaps and bounds beyond plain water. To bump up the flavor, remove the bones after 45 minutes and then simmer the broth for another 30 minutes to concentrate the flavor. From the bones, remove any remaining meat and set aside to add to the soup.

Rinds from hard cheeses such as Parmigiano-Reggiano can be saved and frozen, and when you have at least 8 ounces, simmer them in several cups of water for any Italian-themed soup. Also, scraps of vegetables which would normally go into the compost or trash can be covered with water and simmered to make a vegetarian broth.

As for using leftovers – choose three things from your fridge that sound like they will go together. Three items will help you retain a focus on what goes well together, and choosing only three items increases the likelihood that you won't end up with an unsavory "everything-but-the-kitchen-sink" soup. What's in my fridge right now that I could make into soup? Mashed potatoes, roasted whole chicken, and kale with onion and tomatoes; or pan-fried fish, julienned veggies sautéed in soy, and some miso; or cilantro and tomato salsa, chili rubbed steak and roasted portabella mushrooms. Of course these are just examples; you won't have these exact combinations sitting idly in your fridge, nor am I suggesting that you should. But they do sound as if they would make excellent soups (and they probably will over the next several days!).

The next step is to sauté one or two chopped onions, minced garlic (and bacon, if you so choose), in butter or olive oil. Sauté them well with salt and pepper until the onions are very soft and translucent. Add perhaps a little tomato paste, a splash of red or white wine (red for tomato-based soups and white for creamy soups). Then add your broth and bring to a simmer. At this point you might choose to add some orzo, leftover rice or diced potatoes for flavor, filler and as a thickening agent. Add the rest of your ingredients and bring to a simmer again, checking for seasoning and doneness of all ingredients. Add a loaf of crusty bread, good butter and a salad and you've got a rich, hearty soup from a little more than a couple of onions and some "leftovers."

February

Comfort food is about the approachable, the straightforward, and the familiar. Nothing unusual, "foo-foo," or adventurous shall pass our lips when responding to a yearning for the cozy and comforting on our plates. There are many times when I (and my family) need this ease, soothing, care and comfort and it can't be found in Shrimp Cocktail over Grapefruit and Fennel Gratina or some such thing. It's the pot roast and pasta that speak to us all; and for what we reach when we're in need of some food for the soul.

Fettuccini with Chicken, Mushrooms and Caramelized Onions

This recipe is perfect for using up leftovers from a whole roasted chicken. If you don't have cooked chicken handy, you can use uncooked, boneless chicken – 1 to 1 1/2 pounds of chicken tenders, breasts, or thighs, cut into 1/4-inch slices. Just add the chicken at the same time as the mushrooms instead of at the end of the recipe and increase the cooking time to 10 minutes. Serves 4 to 6 generously

1 pound fettuccini
2 tablespoons olive oil
3 cups sliced onions; about 2 small to medium onions
10 ounces mushrooms, sliced; about 4 cups
1 1/2 teaspoons kosher salt
several grinds fresh black pepper
1/2 cup white wine
1 cup heavy cream
3 cups cooked chicken, pulled into 1-inch pieces
1/2 cup grated Parmesan cheese

Following the instructions on the package, bring water for the fettuccini to a boil. While the water is heating, heat the oil in a large sauté pan over medium-high heat; once the oil is hot, add the onions. Sauté the onions for 20 minutes, reducing heat to medium-low when the pan begins to brown slightly. When the onions are tender and golden brown, add the mushrooms, salt, and pepper and sauté for another 5 minutes. Add the wine, return the heat to medium-high and bring to a boil. Begin cooking the pasta following the package instructions. Add the heavy cream to the onion/mushroom pan and bring to a boil again. Add the chicken and continue cooking for a few more minutes, stirring frequently, until the chicken is heated through; serve over the pasta with Parmesan as a garnish.

Homemade Chicken Nuggets with Blue Cheese Dipping Sauce

Serve these crispy chicken bites with carrot and celery sticks; a simple Romaine salad and homemade Blue Cheese Dipping Sauce. Have some Frank's RedHot Sauce on the side if you want to spice things up, and/or honey if you like the sweeter side of life. Serves 4 to 6

Nuggets
1/2 cup buttermilk
1 tablespoon Frank's RedHot sauce (or more)

1 teaspoon kosher salt
1 1/2 pounds chicken tenderloins (chicken tenders)
1 cup Panko bread crumbs

Blue Cheese Dipping Sauce
5 ounces crumbled blue cheese; about 1 cup
1/2 cup buttermilk
1/2 cup mayonnaise
1/2 teaspoon minced garlic; about 1 clove
several grinds fresh black pepper

4 medium to large carrots, cut into 3-inch sticks
2 large celery sticks, cut into 3-inch sticks

Nuggets
Preheat the broiler. Line a rimmed baking sheet with foil, and then place two cooling racks (the ones you usually use for cooling cookies), side-by-side and over lapping,
on the baking sheet. In a medium bowl, whisk the buttermilk, hot sauce and salt. Add
the chicken and with a wooden spoon or your hands, turning to coat. Place the bread
crumbs in a medium bowl and dredge the chicken in the crumbs. Place the chicken on
the prepared baking sheet. Broil for 4 to 6 minutes on each side, turning with tongs when
the edges begin to brown. You'll need to watch these carefully as under the broiler things
can go from 0 to 60 mph pretty quickly. Cooking times will vary with the thickness of the
tenders. Serve with carrot and celery sticks and blue cheese sauce.

Blue Cheese Dipping Sauce
Meanwhile, combine all of the sauce ingredients in a medium bowl and whisk until the
blue cheese has been broken into pea size or smaller pieces.

Homemade Macaroni and Cheese

*To this basic recipe I add one-squillion different ingredients, my favorite of which are spinach and toma-
toes; pancetta and kale; or broccoli and chicken. This is better when served fresh out of the oven as the
longer it sits, the more the pasta soaks up the sauce leaving things a little stiff for my taste.* Serves 6 to 8

1 pound penne or other pasta, undercooked
1/4 cup unsalted butter (1/2 stick) plus a little extra for the casserole dish
2 cups diced onions; about 1 medium onion
1/4 cup all-purpose flour
2 teaspoons salt
several grinds of white pepper (or black if you don't mind seeing the black flecks)

7 cups whole milk

4 ounces grated Parmesan cheese; about 2 cups

4 ounces grated Cheddar cheese; about 2 cups

Crumb Topping

1/4 cup butter (1/2 stick), melted

1 cup bread crumbs

Preheat oven to 375 degrees. In a medium stockpot (or the pot you used to cook the pasta), melt the butter over medium-high heat. Add the onion and sauté until translucent, about 10 minutes. Add the flour, salt and pepper and stir until fully incorporated. Whisk the milk in briskly and bring to a simmer, whisking often. Remove from heat and add the pasta and stir with a wooden spoon. Add the cheeses, stirring until melted and the wooden spoon is fully coated with the sauce. Transfer to a buttered 3-quart casserole. In a small bowl, combine the crumb topping ingredients and sprinkle over the pasta. Bake for 45 minutes to 1 hour or until the edges are bubbly and brown and the center is fully hot.

Chili-Rubbed Pot Roast with Browned Onion Relish

This pot roast can be served hot or cold as a pot luck or buffet brunch dish. The small amount of cinnamon in this rub goes well with the other spices and will meld into the meat rather than be a distinguishable flavor. Give it a try. This is a cut that benefits from low and slow heat which allows the sinew to be bathed by slowly melting collagen, which is a technical explanation for tender and delicious! This pot roast is also good slathered with a hot tomato chutney or a grainy mustard. Serves 6 to 8

1 1/2 teaspoons kosher salt

1/4 teaspoon freshly ground black pepper

1/2 teaspoon ground paprika

1/2 teaspoon ground cinnamon

2 teaspoons chili powder

2 teaspoons ground cumin

1 (3 to 4 pound) chuck roast

1 tablespoon canola oil

4 cups onion, peeled and cut into 1-inch chunks; about 3 medium onions

2 whole heads garlic, excess skin removed and very top cut off

1 cup red wine

2 cups beef broth

1 or 2 teaspoons balsamic vinegar

Combine salt, pepper, spices and oil in a small bowl. Rub the roast two hours ahead of time or overnight with both the oil and the spices.

Preheat oven to 300 degrees. Heat a large Dutch oven over medium-high heat and brown the roast on all sides, about 10 minutes. Add the onions to the pot and sauté until they also begin to brown, about 7 to 10 minutes. Add the garlic, red wine and broth and cover. Transfer to oven and cook for 3 to 4 hours or until the onions are a very deep brown, the liquid is nearly entirely reduced and the meat is very tender.

Carefully transfer the meat to a cutting board and let rest for at least 15 minutes. If you still have liquid in the bottom of the pan, remove the garlic heads and return the pan to the stove top and reduce until the onions are more of a paste, about 15 to 30 minutes. To the pan of onions, add 1 to 2 teaspoons of balsamic vinegar to taste. Spoon relish into small serving bowl. At this point, you can do one of two things; either slice immediately and serve hot, or cool and slice for sandwiches or a buffet.

LAYING THE FOUNDATION
Sourdough - Experiment & Tradition

Sometimes I wonder at the leap of faith it must have taken for that first person to discover that while wine left too long became unpalatable, if left even longer, would become palatable again as vinegar. Or that flour and water, when mixed together then left alone, would take on a life of its own amidst a bubble of bacterial activity. And who was brave enough, discerning enough, or hungry enough to discover that the gooey, sour mess is actually a delight when combined with flour, salt and water, and then baked into bread?

The sourdough starter that I've used for the past decade or so was given to me by a guest who also happened to be a chef. He claimed that his starter was over 100 years old and had traveled west with the early settlers, then returned back east via his grandmother. With its rich smell and mellow flavor, I have every reason to believe him. Because it's so precious to me, I've frozen a couple of batches just in case something goes terribly awry and I lose my working starter. It's more an insurance policy than a likelihood; what's more likely is that my well-fed starter will take over the galley in its zeal to consume starch.

My journey of discovery into bread making, and sourdough bread making in particular, was a combination of science, art, and good timing. I received the gift of the sourdough starter right around the same time I was experimenting with no-knead baking. The combination of sourdough starter, my quest for a no-knead bread, the challenges of working in a small, small, small cooking space, and my desire for creativity all merged together. The result? Not so much a recipe as a template for bread baking that produces loaf after loaf of creative, delicious breads.

Instead of using sourdough as a leavening, I use it primarily for flavor. While it does add to the leavening of my bread, I don't depend upon the sourdough alone; I also use yeast to insure consistency and to shorten the rising and/or resting time. This also allows for a higher moisture content which makes for a terrific crust and a moist interior.

The best part is that I can now incorporate all sorts of leftover grains into my bread with ease and consistency. Brown rice, oatmeal, millet, quinoa and polenta all find a second life in my healthy breads.

So this is how it works:

1. In a large bowl, mix together a ratio of:
   5 cups flour (or flours) of your choice
   1 tablespoon yeast
   1 tablespoon salt

2. Add 1 to 2 cups of cooked grain such as brown rice, oatmeal, millet, quinoa or polenta.

3. Then add 1/2 to 1 cup of flavoring ingredients such as olives, dried fruit, roasted red peppers, etc.

4. Also add any herbs or spices – around 2 teaspoons of dried or 1/4 cup freshly chopped herbs.

5. Add 1 cup sourdough starter; begin to mix everything together with your hands.

6. Add water and continue to mix, adding water, until the dough just barely forms a ball and there are no little dry bits hanging out in the bowl. Depending on how moist the cooked grain is, the amount of water can vary from 1/2 cup to 2 cups.

7. Cover the bowl with a layer of plastic wrap; and let the dough rise at room temperature for 1 to 2 hours, until the surface of the dough has risen and is flat, not rounded. For those who have worked with traditional kneaded dough, this will look like a disaster. Just wait, it will be fine.

8. Put the dough into the refrigerator for at least 2 hours or overnight. No need to punch it down, in any event, it will look too loose for that.

9. Preheat the oven to 450 degrees. Place a heavy (empty) pan or skillet in the bottom of the oven (you'll use this when you put your bread in the oven to create steam). I use a cast iron skillet, filled with rocks I've picked from the garden and scrubbed clean, to create a sauna of sorts. It just stays in the oven all the time. The addition of moisture into the oven air helps the bread rise more and then creates a terrific crust.

10. Shape the dough into the loaves of your choice - 3 baguettes, 2 batons or 1 large boule. Do this by turning the dough onto a floured surface, cutting into the number of pieces you need and gently turning the edges under to form the desired shape. Sprinkle a baking sheet with corn meal or rice flour and place the loaf/loaves on the baking sheet.

11. Cover with plastic wrap and let the dough rise again for another 20 to 45 minutes depending on the size and looseness of your loaf/loaves.

12. Slash the tops of the loaf/loaves with a sharp knife, transfer the baking sheet to the oven and immediately pour a cup of warm water into the pan on the bottom of the oven to create the aforementioned steam. Be extra careful with this step and quickly remove your arm from the oven once you've poured the water.

13. Bake until the exterior is golden brown and the bottom is firm, from 25 to 40 minutes depending on the size of your loaf/loaves.

Dutch Oven Bread

Another way to achieve a similar result is to bake your bread in a Dutch oven. This covered pot creates a convective space for moist air, which allows the bread to rise beautifully, and then, once the moisture has dissipated, creates a terrific crust. I use this method at home frequently. However, on the *Riggin* I need to make 4 loaves at a time – but I don't have the space for 4 Dutch ovens. So I choose the first, more traditional method. To make the Dutch Oven Bread variation, follow steps 1 through 8, then:

1. Place a covered Dutch oven into the unheated oven. Preheat oven to 450 degrees.

2. Shape the dough into a round boule; place the loaf in a bowl lined with parchment paper.

3. Cover the bowl with plastic wrap and let the dough rise again until doubled, another 45 minutes to 1 hour.

4. Slash the tops of the loaf with a sharp knife and transfer the parchment paper and dough to the hot Dutch oven and cover with the hot lid.

5. Bake until the exterior is golden brown and the bottom is firm; about 50 to 70 minutes (no peaking for at least the first half hour). Remove from both the oven and the Dutch oven and let cool before slicing.

Space only allows for so much in a printed book, however, the blog has much more detail on sourdough and how I use it should you be interested in more information. www.athomeatsea.com

March

Greens! Dark, bitter, full of vitamins, minerals and goodness - they bring color to an otherwise drab time of year. The flowers aren't blooming yet and the trees are still dormant. The mud, however, is alive and well and our mud boots are a common sight, waiting by the back door, like little faithful soldiers ready for action. I pull them on often to tramp out to the garden to cut our greens for dinner; miraculously, they're thriving underneath my cold frames. What a spirit lift it is to begin harvesting in March!

Thai-Inspired Maine Shrimp Cakes

If you'd like to serve these as an appetizer, simply make smaller cakes and reduce the cooking time some. Pacific shrimp can be substituted for the Maine shrimp, just be sure to remove the peel and the tails before chopping. Serves 4 to 6; makes 8 to 12 cakes

1 teaspoon minced garlic; about 1 clove
3/4 pound peeled, uncooked Maine shrimp, coarsely chopped
1 1/2 cups cooked jasmine rice
2 teaspoons minced fresh basil
2 teaspoons minced fresh mint
2 teaspoons minced fresh cilantro
2 teaspoons Sriracha or other hot sauce
2 egg whites
4 tablespoons extra virgin olive oil
1/4 cup finely sliced scallions for garnish

Combine all ingredients except olive oil and scallions in a medium sized bowl. Using your hands, scoop enough of the mixture to make a 1 to 1 1/2-inch ball just as you would a meatball. Heat a large skillet over medium-high heat and add half of the oil. Press the balls into the pan, flattening them into cakes, and cook for 4 minutes or until crispy and lightly browned. Flip with a spatula and brown the other side. Be sure to leave space in the pan between each cake so that they have enough heat to brown well.

Repeat until all of the cakes are cooked using the rest of the oil as needed. Serve immediately with Yogurt Chive Sauce (page 14) or Chive and Tomato Garnish (page 119).

Scallops with Black Bean, Avocado and Goat Cheese Salad

Serves 4

Black Beans
2 (16-ounce) cans black beans, lightly rinsed
1 avocado, peeled, seeded and diced
6 ounces crumbled goat cheese
2/3 cup diced red pepper, cored and seeded; a little less than 1 pepper
1/4 cup minced red onion; about 1/4 of an onion
2 tablespoons minced fresh cilantro
1 teaspoon minced jalapeno pepper, cored and seeded (optional)

3/4 teaspoon kosher salt
4 tablespoons extra virgin olive oil
2 tablespoons lime juice; about 1/2 a lime
8 medium sized romaine leaves, rinsed and patted dry

Scallops
3/4 pound scallops, muscle removed
1/2 teaspoon red pepper flakes
2 teaspoons lime juice
2 teaspoons minced garlic; about 2 cloves
4 teaspoons extra virgin olive oil, plus one more teaspoon for the pan
1/2 teaspoon kosher salt

Black Beans
In a medium bowl, combine all ingredients except the romaine and stir to incorporate.
Lay 2 romaine leaves per person on a plate. Spoon the black bean mix over the base of
the leaves, dividing evenly. With tongs, transfer the cooked scallops on top of the black
bean mix and serve immediately.

Scallops
Combine all ingredients and marinate the scallops for at least 10 minutes and up to several hours before cooking. Heat a large skillet over medium high heat. Add oil to the pan,
barely coating the bottom. Transfer the scallops to the hot skillet with tongs, leaving space
between each scallop. Cook for 2 to 3 minutes each side. The scallops are done just before
the center turns white. They cook very quickly and will continue to cook once removed
from the pan. Transfer immediately to the top of the black beans.

Pan-Fried Monkfish

*If you have hungry people to serve, you could add another 1/2 to 1 pound of fish, but the medallions
stretch it a bit and with a hearty side of potatoes or rice, 1 pound of monkfish serves 4 perfectly.*

*Monkfish is pretty easy to find in our area, however, if you have trouble, substitute any firm-fleshed white
fish like grouper or halibut in its place.* Serves 4

1 pound monkfish, trimmed
1 cup all-purpose flour
3 tablespoons extra virgin olive oil
kosher salt to sprinkle
several grinds fresh black pepper
1 lime cut into wedges for garnish

Cut the monkfish into 1/2-inch medallions and gently, with the flat of a tenderizing mallet or other heavy object, flatten to 1/4-inch thickness. Place flour on a platter and dredge the fish medallions in the flour. Heat a skillet over medium-high heat and add the oil. Carefully add the medallions to the skillet, sprinkle with salt and pepper and fry for about 2 minutes each side. Serve over Spinach and Lime Confetti Salad (page 116) with lime wedges as a garnish and with a side of potatoes or rice if you wish.

Mussels with Chorizo and Red Wine

I've found a local source for chorizo recently and have been using it with abandon ever since. Mussels are a perfect weeknight meal because they are quick cooking — very little standing over the stove for these savory numbers — yet still richly satisfying.

Crusty bread to sop up the cooking liquid is a must. This recipe can be easily doubled or tripled for entertaining. Serves 2 as a main course or 4 as an appetizer

2 tablespoons extra virgin olive oil
1 tablespoon minced garlic, about 2 cloves
4 ounces diced Spanish (dry-cured) chorizo, casing removed beforehand; about 1 cup
1/2 teaspoon pimentón or paprika
1/2 teaspoon salt
1/4 cup red wine
1 pound mussels, in-shell, washed and de-bearded

In a large stockpot, heat the oil over medium high heat. Add the garlic and sauté for 30 seconds to 1 minute. Add the chorizo and pimentón and sauté for another minute or two. Add the mussels and the rest of the ingredients. Cover and steam until the mussels open fully, another 2 to 3 minutes.

LET'S GROW
Extending the Season, Cold Frames, Greenhouse

Living in Maine, loving to garden, and committing to eating as much locally grown, organic produce as possible means we, and the local farms around us, will do anything to help extend our short growing season. I've tried myriad methods, from simple straw bale cold frames to a complete greenhouse, each of which comes with its own level of complexity, drawbacks, and advantages. Each of the methods listed below, except for our small greenhouse, fits over a 4' x 8' raised bed inside our fenced-in garden.

Raised beds are simply boxes that rest on the ground and hold soil within the box and a way of organizing the garden and pathways in a more defined manner. They warm up faster in the spring and, in our garden, allow for better drainage of the soil as our water table is fairly high.

Straw Bale Frame

This is the easiest, cheapest and least permanent method of extending the growing season. Four bales, flakes broken apart and stacked, will easily surround a 4' x 8' raised bed and give a little height to the plastic which covers the bed. For the cover I've used sliding glass doors, old windows, sheets of plastic, firm Plexiglas and row covers. Plastic sheets combined with a row cover beneath it works as well as anything, provided you secure the edges well. The sliding glass doors were the most effective, but with our girls traipsing around the garden, the idea that one of them might lose their balance and fall onto the glass led us to discarding that plan. It's important to use the slightly more expensive straw, not hay, for it is devoid of weed seeds (unlike hay) and won't haunt you with new weeds for seasons to come.

Hoop House

Elliot Coleman is the man who deserves the credit for this one. The author of *Four Season Harvest*, his innovative thinking about cold season gardening and his own personal success with growing greens all winter is inspiring. The hoops are made of electrical conduit, bent over the width of the bed which creates about a 3-foot-high arch over the soil. The hoops are then covered with two layers of 6 mil plastic, anchored very securely on all sides with either rocks, sand bags or 2 x 4's, and supported with strapping secured lengthwise. To secure the sides with 2 x 4's, we take the long sides of the plastic, sandwich the two layers between two lengths of strapping or 2 x 4's, secure the "sandwich" with sheet rock screws and roll it up onto itself. On warm spring days, the roll of sandwiched plastic can be hiked up to the centerline to cool off the bed. In winter months, this is the most effective way to keep the edges down and out of reach of the wind's diligent hands, which are apt to get a pinky hold on a corner of plastic and work the whole sheet free. This is most likely to occur on the windiest and snowiest day of the winter when you are least interested in traipsing out to save your lettuce. Instead, protect your lettuce by preparing for those windy days ahead of time. The short ends are then secured with heavy bricks and rocks.

Cold Frame

For a building project, this is a fairly simple one, although it does require some basic knowledge of tools and hardware. My cold frame is simply a raised bed with an angle to it so that more surface area can face the sun. The lid is built with strapping and supports so that two sheets of plastic can be stretched and secured firmly across the top. The lid is hinged and lifts as one unit and is secured by a simple hook and eye to guard against blowing open on those extremely windy days. Ply-wood or 2 x 12's can make up the angled side pieces which provide the opportunity to catch more sun and heat.

Mini-Greenhouse

This is the sturdiest, most effective and durable of all of the methods I've used – and also the hardest to build. There is no way I could have finished it without Jon's help. I started the project with all of my usual optimism, but without his constant support, it was beyond my skill level. That said, I love it. It's easy to get into, heats faster, stays warm longer and therefore grows my veggies better than the others. It's also really heavy; every time I want to move it to another raised bed, I need three other people to help move it –something else to consider when you are choosing a design. However, from a strictly visual perspective, it is the most pleasing and beautiful to see either up close or from afar; and it doesn't hurt my overdeveloped sense of frugality that it uses 6 recycled doubled-paned windows for the access points.

Full-sized Greenhouse

What can I say? I love it. It was a gift from the girls and Jon for Mother's Day last year and something I've wanted since I began gardening almost 20 years ago. It must be said that due to the fact that there is so much head room, the insulating value of the greenhouse isn't as great as any of the above methods which simply cover the raised beds. The early seedlings I planted this year came up and then were zapped by a 20 degree frost which is common before we hit the end of April. Next time I'll be sure to cover them entirely with plastic so that the ground can become warmer sooner and the seedlings can have more insulation.

Using recycled material - old storm windows, reclaimed wood, scrap pieces of ply-wood - is a good way to use up those pieces lying around the basement or garage and to reduce the cost of a season extending frame.

April

There's something very satisfying about making things from scratch. Whether it's an apron, a felted trivet, ricotta gnocchi or my own vanilla extract, the feeling of accomplishment and self-sufficiency gives me a sense of mastery over my little realm – even if it is a pretty small space!

Ricotta Gnocchi

If you use homemade ricotta for this recipe, the water content may vary. In this case, either strain the ricotta for 30 minutes in cheesecloth, or if it's drier than the commercial varieties, add a little milk.

This recipe is similar to that in "A16: Food + Wine" by Nate Appleman. I've made many adjustments, of course, but his cooking inspires me, and it's always important to give credit to the idea. Serves 4 to 6

2 cups whole milk ricotta cheese
2 tablespoons extra virgin olive oil
3/4 teaspoon kosher salt
1 egg
1 egg yolk
2 cups all-purpose flour
1/4 cup semolina flour; more if needed

Bring a large pot of salted water to boil while you make the gnocchi. While the water is heating, whisk the ricotta, olive oil and salt with either a stand mixer or hand mixer until the ricotta is smooth and the large lumps have dissolved, about 1 minute. Add the egg and egg yolk and whisk again to incorporate.

Make a mound of the all-purpose flour on the counter. With your hands, make a well in the center and scrape the ricotta mixture into the well with a spatula. With a bench scraper, fold the flour into the ricotta using a scraping motion and then a chopping or cutting motion on the top. Continue to scrape and chop until the flour is just incorporated. Be sure to not work the dough too much as this will result in tough gnocchi. To test for texture and whether the gnocchi have enough flour, take several pinches of dough and form them into small balls. Drop them into the boiling water to check for the dough structure. Wait until they float to the top and cook for another 2 minutes or so. If they fall apart a bit, add a little more flour to the dough.

Cut the dough into 4 separate pieces and sprinkle the counter with some of the semolina flour. With your hands, roll the dough into a long tube just as if you were making mud worms like a child. They should be about 1/2-inch in diameter.

Repeat with the other three pieces of dough and then roll the logs close to each other. Using the bench scraper, a knife or a pizza cutter, cut the logs into 1/2-inch sized pieces. Sprinkle them with more semolina.

At this point you can freeze them on a sheet pan lightly dusted with semolina. Once they are frozen, transfer to an air tight container.

Or, if you are ready to use them immediately, prepare the rest of your ingredients and when everything else is set, transfer the gnocchi to the boiling water. Stir well and watch for them to float to the surface. Cook for another 2 to 3 minutes and drain reserving 1/2 cup of the water for the sausage and broccoli raab. Serve with Chicken, Basil and Sundried Tomato Sausage and Broccoli Raab (page 48).

If your gnocchi are frozen, add them to boiling water without defrosting and increase cooking time by 3 to 5 minutes.

Chicken, Basil and Sun-dried Tomato Sausage with Broccoli Raab over Ricotta Gnocchi

If you can't find broccoli raab, spinach makes a good substitute. Use about 4 cups spinach (about 5 ounces) in place of the broccoli raab. If you use spinach instead, don't blanch before adding it to the sausage but simply add it directly.

If you have any leftovers, this makes a terrific soup the following day with the addition of a can of fire roasted tomatoes. Add the leftovers to a pot and cover generously with chicken broth and the tomatoes. Bring to a boil and serve with grated Asiago cheese as a garnish. Serves 4 to 6

10 ounces broccoli raab, stem ends removed and chopped into 1 to 2-inch lengths
3 tablespoons olive oil (2 for cooking the sausage, 1 to drizzle on the gnocchi at the end)
1 pound Chicken, Basil and Sun-dried Tomato Sausage (page 49) or sweet Italian sausage, casing removed
1 cup red onion, peeled and sliced; about 1/2 an onion
1/2 yellow bell pepper, cored, seeded and sliced; about 1 cup
1 1/2 tablespoons minced garlic; about 3 cloves
1 teaspoon kosher salt
several grinds fresh black pepper
zest from one lemon
3/4 cup grated Asiago cheese
1 Ricotta Gnocchi recipe (page 46)
2 to 4 tablespoons of the gnocchi water

Bring a large pot of salted water to a boil. Drop the broccoli raab into the boiling water and blanch for 2 to 3 minutes. This leaches out some of the bitterness, but the point is not to cook them all the way through. Remove from the water with a slotted spoon or basket strainer and set aside. Reuse the same pot of water to cook the gnocchi when you are ready.

Heat a large skillet over medium-high heat and add the olive oil. On one side of the pan add the sausage and the other, the onions. Use tongs to break up the sausage and to stir the onions. When the onions are beginning to turn brown on the edges, about 7 to 10 minutes, add the peppers on top of the onions and stir. When the peppers are tender but still firm, about 4 minutes, make a well in the sausage and add the garlic to the well; this uses the fat from the sausage to help sauté the garlic. Sauté an additional 30 seconds to one minute and then mix it all together, adding the salt, pepper and lemon zest. Add the broccoli raab, turn with tongs and remove from heat. Add the reserved gnocchi water to loosen the sauce if needed.

When the gnocchi are done, add them to the skillet to combine with the broccoli raab and sausage, or serve the gnocchi on a platter topped with the sausage and broccoli raab. Garnish with Asiago.

Chicken, Basil and Sun-dried Tomato Sausage

I like to keep this recipe doubled and freeze half for the future to use in tacos, with eggs or over a pasta dish. Feel free to halve it should you only wish to use it with the broccoli raab recipe. Makes about 4 cups of sausage

2 pounds boneless, skinless chicken thighs, cut into 1-inch pieces, fat included
2 ounces grated Parmesan cheese; about 1 cup
2 teaspoons minced garlic; about 2 cloves
1/4 cup coarsely chopped fresh basil
1/4 cup sun-dried tomatoes in oil
1/2 teaspoon kosher salt
1/4 teaspoon freshly ground black pepper

Freeze the chicken for 30 minutes. This will help it run through the grinder more easily. Combine all ingredients and work together with your hands. Following the directions for your grinder, coarsely grind the mixture in small batches. Wrap half of the mixture in plastic wrap and freeze for up to 3 months.

Baked Gnocchi with Garlic and Cream

The sublime creaminess of this satisfying dish is beautifully offset by slightly pungent and bitter accents of broccoli raab or kale. This is a great way to use up leftover gnocchi from a previous meal. Refrigerating them gives the dumplings a chance to set up a bit and stand up to the cream and the baking instead of falling apart. Of course you can always use store-bought gnocchi as well - the whole wheat are especially nice. Serves 4 to 6

1 pound homemade ricotta gnocchi (or store-bought whole wheat gnocchi)
6 cloves whole garlic
1/2 teaspoon kosher salt
1 cup heavy cream
1 cup grated Parmesan cheese

Preheat oven to 375 degrees. Combine all ingredients and transfer to a 10-inch deep-dish pie plate. Bake for 40 to 45 minutes or until the edges are bubbly and the cream has thickened in the center. Serve immediately.

STOCK UP
Bourbon Vanilla, Granola, & Dulce de Leche

Sometimes what's stored in my pantry makes all the difference between something good and something great. Take vanilla extract for example. Shortbread made with homemade bourbon vanilla instead of store-bought vanilla extract is a treat that ranks high on my list of all-time favorite desserts. Of course, while I like shortbread well enough, I'm just as likely to pass on it for something chocolate unless it's made with homemade bourbon vanilla extract; say, perhaps, two chocolate wafers sandwiched with dulce de leche and sprinkled with sea salt. Or frozen yogurt drizzled with honey and sprinkled with granola.

While each of these concoctions – bourbon vanilla, granola, and dulce de leche – are worthy of appreciation in their own right, they also serve as a foundation for a well-stocked pantry which, in turn, builds dishes packed with flavor, quick solutions for an evening's entertainment, and even home-made gifts.

Homemade Bourbon Vanilla

Because I use so much vanilla extract when baking over the summer, I've found it easier, more economical, and much more flavorful to make my own. I make it in the spring to use all summer long. Even if you don't use vanilla every day like I do, searching for vanilla beans in bulk and adding them to a small amount of bourbon or vodka is a money-saver long term. This is also a perfect use for older vanilla beans – the ones that are dry and difficult to split. It's what I do with any vanilla beans left over from the previous summer's cruises. They will swell up just like fresh, pliant beans after a soak in the bourbon and there is no difference in the end result.

Bourbon Vanilla is easy to make. Split 6 vanilla beans (lengthwise, to expose the seeds). Pop them into a 1.75-liter bottle of mid-shelf bourbon, recap the bottle, put it in the back of your pantry for 6 weeks (shake every so often), and Ta Da! Bourbon Vanilla. Once the vanilla is gone, I shake the beans out of the bottle and use the seeds or beans to flavor sugar, custards and desserts. The beans, swollen with alcohol, will last a long while, although they are so versatile that they don't stick around for long. Decanted into smaller, pretty bottles, this vanilla also makes for good gifts at Christmas time.

Cinnamon Pecan Granola

Sure you can buy it in every grocery store in the country, but it's easy to make for yourself and smells delicious while you're baking it! Makes 12 cups

1/3 cup canola oil
2/3 cup honey
2 teaspoons vanilla extract (or Bourbon Vanilla see page 50)
2 cups unsweetened shredded coconut
1 cup chopped pecans
8 cups whole rolled oats
2 teaspoons ground cinnamon

Preheat oven to 325 degrees. Heat the honey and oil together in a small saucepan. Add the vanilla. In a large bowl, add all of the dry ingredients and toss them all together with the warm honey and oil mixture until well-mixed. Transfer to a rimmed baking sheet. Bake for 45 minutes to 1 hour or until the color has changed to a golden brown. You'll need to stir occasionally for even browning, and to prevent clumping. Let cool completely and then store in an airtight container

Granny Joan's Blueberry-Cranberry Granola

When guests came to visit, this granola was in the oven cooking and the house smelled so inviting. The next morning, we had it for breakfast with yogurt and fruit and Granny Joan couldn't believe how yummy it was and good for us too! I have to say that I do think it's the height of unfairness that the only granola recipes that don't taste like twigs, also have more than their fair share of sugar, but there you have it. Makes approximately 16 cups

1/2 cup honey
1/2 cup maple syrup
1/2 cup canola oil
2 teaspoons vanilla extract (or Bourbon Vanilla see page 50)
6 cups whole old-fashioned oats
1 1/2 cups wheat germ
1 1/2 cups sliced almonds
1 cup packed light brown sugar
2 cups unsweetened shredded coconut
3/4 cup sesame seeds
1/2 cup hulled sunflower seeds
1 cup ground flax seeds
2 cups bran cereal (not the flakes but the stick kind)

1 cup dried powdered milk
1 cup unsweetened dried blueberries
1 cup unsweetened dried cranberries

Preheat oven to 325 degrees. Heat the honey, maple syrup and canola oil in a small saucepan. Add the vanilla. In a large bowl, add all of the dry ingredients and toss them all together with the warm honey and oil mixture until well-mixed. Transfer to a rimmed baking sheet. Bake for 45 minutes to 1 hour or until the color has changed to a golden brown. You'll need to stir occasionally for even browning, and to prevent clumping. Let cool completely, add the blueberries and cranberries and then store in an airtight container.

Dulce de Leche

This is one of those deceptively simple, utterly delicious concoctions that comes from, most notably, Argentina. In Mexico it is made with goat's milk rather than cow's milk. Translated, it means 'sweet [made] of milk.' In France it's called confiture de lait.

The transformation from white liquid to caramel brown spread is caused by two chemical reactions – caramelization and the Maillard reaction. The result is heaven on a spoon.

This is one of my staples; it can be used for making ice cream or muffins, as the center for wafer cookies, and any number of special desserts. My girls like to have it as an afternoon snack, spread over fresh baguettes so it often doesn't last long enough to make it into a dessert. Makes 1 cup

2 cups heavy cream
1/3 cup sugar
pinch of sea salt
pinch of baking soda

Combine all ingredients with a wooden spoon in a small, heavy-duty saucepan over medium-high heat. Bring to a full boil and then reduce the heat to low. Cook for up to 1 hour or until the color begins to change to a beige/light caramel. Transfer immediately to a cool bowl to stop the cooking process. Once it's cooled completely store in a jar in the fridge for up to 3 months, although I guarantee it won't last that long!

The sky is the limit when it comes to changing a granola recipe. Some of my *other* favorite combinations are Cashew and Apricot; Cranberry and Ginger or a Hawaiian with Pineapple, Mango and Macadamia Nuts. All the fruit is dried of course.

May

The gardens, the boat, the girls, the house,
the chickens, the bees, oh my! May is a
very busy month for us - one where we
shift our entire focus from land to sea. In
the spring, our schedule blooms to life just
as the bulbs in the garden begin to show
their brilliant colors and the trees turn to
a sea of lime-pea-Kelly -chartreuse-green.
As the weather moves through predictable
rainy then sunny patterns, we haul the
Riggin out of the water, hoping for one of
the sunny times. And then the lilacs bloom.
And then we go sailing. A pattern repeats.

ON DECK WITH CAPT. JON
Haul-Out

Haul-out. It's a fascinating process in which a massive 75-ton, 120-foot (sparred length) schooner is pulled out of its natural environment, the ocean, to have its hull cleaned and painted, only to be returned once again to the cold, briny waters of Penobscot Bay. It's the only time of year that the *Riggin* is completely out of the water. It's also the dirtiest, most grueling three to four days of our entire year, when we work from sun up until after sun down (sometimes by the light of our truck's head lamps) in a race to the finish line – to get off the railway and back in the water on schedule.

Each spring, there are roughly a dozen schooners that need to be hauled out, cleaned, painted, then returned to the water within a very small timeframe – between when the snow is gone and the first cruise begins. Each of these schooners is worked into a precisely constructed schedule. To be unable to launch on time would be at best impolite, and at worst push the last person on the haul-out calendar into their sailing season.

The schedule for the hauling out of schooners in the spring is usually created by Captain John Foss of North End Shipyard in Rockland. North End is where the majority of wind-jammers find themselves laid bare each spring. This schedule depends on the predicted height of the tides and the known draft of the schooners. Schooners with less draft are scheduled during the lower high tides and, as you then might expect, schooners with greater draft are scheduled for the higher tides, where the ocean gives them more room to maneuver. The haul out schedule generally begins April 1st, which is usually when the ice and snow are gone. Usually. We once had 9 inches of snow the night before hauling out in early April; we had to shovel out the shipyard by hand before bringing the *Riggin* over to haul. Sometimes we get lucky, sometimes we don't; hauling out can be numbingly cold when we draw the weather short-straw or delightfully temperate when the weather gods shine upon us.

The Hauling Process
These are large vessels, not small boats, and they require the strength of a shipyard railway to haul them out of the water. A shipyard railway is an angled ramp with a set of large railroad tracks that run down the ramp into the water. A cradle, a simple but strong wood and steel framework which can be moved along the set of railroad tracks into and

then out of the water, receives the schooner. Once the schooner is in the cradle, supports can be placed underneath, and ultimately the cradle and schooner ride up and down the rails together by way of a large winch and wire cable system. The process is ancient – and ingenious.

To prepare for the railway, we must first ready the yawl boat, which provides propulsion for the engineless schooner. The yawl boat is a 16-foot open launch used for moving the vessel on and off the dock, or to push the boat when the winds are light. We use it as a small tug boat. The yawl boat needs to be launched several days ahead of haul-out. Next the crew and I are busy taking down the winter house which covers the vessel with a construction similar to a protective greenhouse. Every part of the winter house gets labeled and stored so it can be used again the following year.

Just before moving the *Riggin* to the shipyard, the crew and I drive to the shipyard, and stack and staple together huge sets of wooden blocks to create several sets of blocking, which support the shape of the *Riggin*'s hull. The blocking rests on the bed of the cradle and, once the vessel is lined up and centered on the cradle, is pulled up against the hull. They keep the *Riggin* upright once the boat's weight is resting on the bed of the cradle.

About a half hour before high tide, the shipyard crew lowers the cradle down the track and into the water as far as it will go. At this time, we have the schooner en route, being pushed by Annie in the yawl boat. We line up the schooner between the raised catwalks of the cradle and slowly come to a stop, making off bow lines, stern lines and spring lines out on both sides of the vessel. Once all the lines are on, we cast off the yawl boat, and follow directions from the shipyard crew, adjusting the lines to get the vessel perfectly lined up over the keel blocking on the cradle (which is now under the boat). A diver is required to make sure everything is lined up just right and that no single part of the hull is bearing too much weight. When everything is lined up just right, the big winch at the top of the ramp is engaged and slowly pulls the cradle up the rails until the bow of the vessel touches the bed of the cradle. When this happens the shipyard crew stops the winch, sends the diver back down to check for proper alignment, then pulls the first set of blocking in to the hull to keep the *Riggin* upright. This slow process of taking up on the winch, checking with the diver etc. continues until all of the stacked blocking is up against the hull and the *Riggin*'s keel is sitting on the bed of the cradle. When the vessel is completely out of the water and above the high tide mark, they stop the winch, set the brake and the job is done. We then set additional supports under the overhanging bow and stern sections.

When the tide recedes, the next three or four (twelve-hour) days are spent power washing barnacles and green slime off the hull; scraping a mussel farm off the bottom with a 2 inch-scraper; sanding the entire hull with a disc sander while perching on less-than-perfectly-constructed scaffolding; and painting 180 linear feet of bottom and then topside of the hull. It's enough to give a person a few sore muscles, a cranky disposition and a longing, not for a bed, but any horizontal surface on which to sleep.

The maintenance is routine. Haul-out happens every year for most of the fleet. And while the work is rhythmic and seasonal and predicted, it is anything but ordinary. For the health of the *Riggin* (or any wooden vessel), the bottom must be painted every year. In addition to painting and all that goes with it, the through-hull fittings must be checked and serviced; seams may need to be re-caulked; and the planking must be surveyed for any changes or deterioration. Should any planks or frames that reside under or close to the water line need replacing, it must be done on the railway. There are also times when a larger body of work is planned that can only be accomplished while on the railway. Much of the time this work is planned and known; of course, there are times when the unexpected happens and we must quickly rethink our plan. Additionally, all passenger schooners undergo hull and safety inspections, and this also needs to be done when the vessel is out of the water.

Finally after the rush of work is completed, the winch at the head of the railway carefully returns the *Riggin* to the sea, the yawl boat is nudged up to a freshly-painted stern, the lines are released, and the *Riggin* is returned to her dock; here we finish the prep work of painting and cleaning before the final rigging and bending on sail in readiness for another season of adventure.

Kale Salad

This salad is an unusual way to serve kale, and is infinitely versatile. The kale will keep much longer in the refrigerator and I find that when I prep kale like this, I end up reaching for it as a base for my lunch salads more often than not. In the wintertime, when I'm wanting something warm to eat, I just add it to a hot skillet for 1 to 2 minutes and then add other vegetables, protein or rice. Serves 6 to 8

12 to 14 ounces kale
1 tablespoon extra virgin olive oil
1 teaspoon kosher salt
several grinds of fresh black pepper
1 tablespoon lemon juice; less than 1/2 a lemon

De-stem the kale and rip it into more manageable 2-inch pieces. Wash in cold water, drain well and pat dry. Drizzle the kale with the olive oil and add the salt and pepper. With your hands, work the oil and salt and pepper into the leaves. When the leaves are fully coated, add the lemon and mix again. Serve as is, add one of the following combinations or your own creation.

Apple, Cranberry and Walnut
Sesame Seeds, Lime, Sesame Oil, Warm Shitake Mushrooms
Pinenuts, Gorgonzola and Fresh Tomatoes

Bright Green Kale with Cranberries and Almonds

Serves 4

12 to 14 ounces kale; about one bunch
2 tablespoons extra virgin olive oil
1/2 teaspoon kosher salt
several grinds fresh black pepper
1/4 cup dried cranberries
1/4 cup sliced almonds

De-stem the kale and rip it into more manageable 2-inch pieces. Wash in cold water and drain. Heat a large skillet over medium-high heat and add the oil. When the oil is hot, remove the pan from the heat and add the kale. Be careful as it will splatter. Turn with tongs and sprinkle with salt and pepper. Continue turning occasionally until the kale is wilted but still very bright green. Taste a leaf to be sure that it's cooked enough that it's not too "toothy," about 4 to 6 minutes. Transfer to a serving bowl or platter and sprinkle with cranberries and almonds.

Swiss Chard with Sesame

Serves 4

2 tablespoons toasted sesame oil
2 cups sliced onions; about 1 large onion
1 bunch Swiss chard; about 6 cups chopped and lightly packed
3 pinches salt
1 tablespoon sesame seeds

Use a knife to separate the chard stems from the leaves by slicing the leaf down each side of the stem. Coarsely chop the leaves and wash and drain well. Chop the stems into 1/2-inch pieces and wash and drain well.

Heat a wok on high heat. Add the oil and swirl to coat the pan. Add the onions and stir-fry until tender and beginning to brown and caramelize. Add the chard stems and stir-fry until tender, about 1 minute. Add the chard leaves and sprinkle with salt and sesame seeds. Stir-fry until the leaves are tender but still bright green, about another minute. Serve over a bed of rice or as a side.

Melty Gouda, Artichoke and Spinach

These two spinach recipes are a snap to make and perfect for those little bits of cheese or meat too small to actually make a meal. Serve with either crostini or crackers. For a warm weeknight meal of wilted salad, omit chopping the spinach, but definitely serve with bread for sopping. Both serve 4 as appetizer

2 ounces grated Gouda cheese; about 1 cup lightly packed
2 ounces coarsely chopped baby spinach; about 2 cups lightly packed
1 (6-ounce) can artichoke hearts, thinly sliced lengthwise
salt and freshly ground pepper
2 tablespoons extra virgin olive oil

Preheat oven to 400 degrees. Combine all ingredients in a medium-sized bowl and transfer to an oven proof platter. Bake for 20 minutes or until the edges are bubbly and the center is melted all the way through.

Melty Hot Sausage, Cheddar and Spinach

1 hot Italian sausage, finely chopped
2 ounces grated Cheddar cheese; about 1 cup lightly packed
2 ounces coarsely chopped baby spinach; about 2 cups lightly packed
salt and freshly ground pepper
1 tablespoon extra virgin olive oil

Preheat oven to 400 degrees. Combine all ingredients in a medium-sized bowl and transfer to an oven proof platter. Bake for 20 minutes or until the edges are bubbly and the center is melted all the way through.

Grilled Snap Peas, Carrots and Radishes

For this recipe you will need either a grill pan or a cast iron skillet which can be placed directly over the grill. Serves 4 to 6

1/2 pound snap peas, ends removed; about 2 cups
1/2 pound carrots, peeled and cut into thin sticks the size of the peas; about 2 cups
1 bunch radishes, ends and tips removed and cut into quarters
3 tablespoons extra virgin olive oil
several pinches kosher salt
several grinds fresh black pepper
Lime and Chive Aioli (page 84)

Make a direct heat fire or heat the grill to medium-high heat. In a large bowl, combine all of the vegetables and coat with oil, salt and pepper. When the fire is ready, place the grill pan or skillet onto the grill and allow to heat, about 3 to 4 minutes. Place the veggies on the grill pan or skillet. Keep a constant eye, moving the veggies around frequently. Remove those that are seared on the outside to the bowl. The peas will be done first, the carrots next and the radishes last.

Serve immediately with Lime and Chive Aioli.

Broccoli with Roasted Red Onion

Serves 4 to 6

2 tablespoons extra virgin olive oil
1 large red onion, core removed and cut into 1/2-inch slices
1/2 teaspoon kosher salt
several grinds of fresh black pepper
8 ounces broccoli cut into large florets; about 1 large head
3 tablespoons lemon juice; about 1/2 a lemon

Heat a medium-sized skillet over medium-high heat. Add the olive oil and then the onions. Sauté the onions until they become soft and begin to brown, about 10 minutes. Reduce heat to medium-low. Sprinkle with salt and pepper, top with broccoli, sprinkle again with salt and pepper and cover for 5 minutes. Remove lid and squeeze the lemon on top of the broccoli. Serve immediately.

Spicy Green Beans and Orange Bell Peppers

Serves 4 to 6

2 tablespoons extra virgin olive oil
1 1/2 teaspoon minced jalapeno or other spicy pepper
1 1/2 teaspoons minced garlic; about 1 large clove
1/2 orange bell pepper, cored, seeded and sliced 1/4-inch thick; about 1 cup
2 pounds green beans, ends removed
2 tablespoons tamari or soy sauce
1 tablespoon Sriracha or other hot sauce

Heat a large skillet over medium-high heat. Add the oil, jalapeno pepper and garlic and sauté for 1 minute. Add the orange pepper and the green beans and sauté for 5 to 7 minutes or until the green beans are tender but still bright green. Season with tamari and Sriracha and serve immediately.

June

It finally happens; the lines are cast off, we're away from the dock, and the sails are set for the first time of the season. It's not until that moment, when I stand on deck with my arms spread wide, face lifted to the sky that I remember why it is that we do what we do. Oftentimes, our crew experiences this same moment. They've spent two or more months sanding and painting every surface of the boat; and in that one moment, we breathe in and shout at the top of our lungs, arms pumping in the air, "We're sailing!"

Chicken, Asparagus and Dill Pot Pie

Serves 6 to 8

3 tablespoons unsalted butter
1 pound boneless, skinless chicken breasts and thighs (or all breasts), cut into 1-inch pieces
2 cups diced onion; about 1 large onion
2 cups peeled and diced carrots; about 2 to 3 carrots
2 cups diced celery; about 2 stalks
1 pound asparagus, ends removed and cut into 3/4-inch pieces; about 1 bunch
1 cup peas, fresh or frozen
2 teaspoons minced fresh dill
3/4 teaspoon kosher salt
1/4 teaspoon freshly ground black pepper
1/3 cup all-purpose flour
3 1/2 cups low-salt chicken broth
1 pie crust recipe (see below)

Preheat oven to 375 degrees. In a medium stockpot over medium high heat, melt the butter and sauté the chicken for 5 to 10 minutes. Add the onions, carrots and celery. When they are soft and translucent, about 10 minutes and then add the asparagus, peas, dill, salt and pepper. Cook for a minute or two and sprinkle the flour on top. Stir and then add the chicken broth. Cook for 30 minutes. Meanwhile line a 9 x 13-inch pan with the bottom crust. When the filling is done, transfer to the pan and cover with the top pie crust. Pinch the edges closed decoratively and bake for 1 hour or until the crust is golden brown and the filling is bubbling on the sides.

Pie Crust

This is a pie crust that I've been using for years; it was the one my mentor, Ellen Barnes, taught me.

If you want to fancy it up a bit, roll out the dough to no less than 1/4-inch thick and place any fresh herbs that you would like on top of the dough. Dill, rosemary, sage, chives, savory, flat leaf parsley and oregano are all nice. Gently roll the leaves into the dough until the dough is no less than 1/8-inch thick. Makes enough for a top and bottom crust for a 9 x 13 pan.

3 cups all-purpose flour
1 1/2 teaspoons salt
3/4 cup (1 1/2 sticks) chilled unsalted butter, cut into 1/2-inch cubes
3/4 cup ice cold water (or more)

Combine the flour, salt, and butter into a medium bowl; cut in well with a pastry knife. Add water and mix until dough pulls away from the bowl and forms a ball. Add more

water if necessary. Divide into two balls, one larger than the other, wrap in plastic wrap and let rest for 30 minutes in the refrigerator.

Roll out the larger ball to 1/4 to 1/8-inch thick in the shape of the pan you are using. Roll out the second ball to the same thickness, an inch or two less in diameter.

Creamy Lemon Asparagus over Whole Wheat Penne

Serves 4 to 6

1 pound whole wheat penne pasta
3 tablespoons unsalted butter
1 1/2 bunches asparagus, ends removed and cut into 1-inch lengths; about 6 cups or 1 1/2 pounds
3/4 teaspoon kosher salt
1/4 teaspoon freshly grated nutmeg
1 1/2 teaspoons lemon zest
1 1/2 cups heavy cream
4 tablespoons lemon juice
1 1/2 cups freshly grated Parmesan cheese

Bring a large pot of salted water to a boil and follow the instructions for the pasta. Meanwhile, heat a large skillet over medium-high heat. Add the butter, then the asparagus and salt. Sauté for 3 to 4 minutes or until the stalks are bright green but still crisp. Add the nutmeg, lemon zest and heavy cream and bring to a boil. Boil for 1 minute and add the lemon juice. Remove from heat, add the cheese and stir. Adjust for salt and let sit while the pasta cooks. Drain the pasta and toss with the sauce. Serve immediately.

Chicken, Asparagus and Basil Soup with Parmesan

Serves 4 to 6

2 tablespoons olive oil
2 pounds chicken breast, cut in half lengthwise and thinly sliced
1 1/2 cups diced onions; about 1 medium onion
1 bunch asparagus, cut into 1/2-inch lengths; about 1 pound
3/4 teaspoon salt

several grinds fresh black pepper
3/4 cup white wine
3 tablespoons minced fresh basil, or 1 tablespoon dried
8 cups low salt chicken broth
1 cup freshly grated Parmesan cheese

Heat a large stockpot over medium-high heat. Add the oil and then the chicken breasts. Sauté until the chicken turns white and is cooked through. Add the onions and sauté for another 10 minutes or until the onions become translucent, about 10 minutes. Add the asparagus, salt and pepper and sauté for another 2 to 3 minutes. Add the wine, basil and chicken broth and bring to a boil. Reduce to a simmer and simmer for 5 minutes. Garnish with Parmesan cheese and serve immediately.

Shaved Asparagus and Arugula Salad with Walnuts

Thinly sliced, asparagus can be served raw and is a delicious way to serve this spring vegetable.

There are two ways to prepare the orange sections. One is simply to peel the orange and separate the sections. The second is to peel the orange with a knife, called supreme or supreming, by slicing off the top and bottom and running your knife between the flesh and the rind. You then run your knife along both sides of the section membranes to remove only the flesh. This is a nicer way to serve the orange, but also a bit more complicated. Choose whichever suits your comfort level. Serves 4 to 6

6 ounces arugula; about 8 cups
1 ounce shaved Romano cheese; about 1/4 cup
1 orange, sectioned, membrane removed, and any juice reserved
2 cups shaved asparagus, about 1 bunch or 15 to 20 stalks
1/2 cup coarsely chopped walnuts
2 tablespoons extra virgin olive oil
2 tablespoons lemon juice; about 1/2 a lemon
2 pinches kosher salt
several grinds fresh black pepper

To shave the asparagus, cut off the flowered tips to 1-inch lengths and reserve. Snap off the ends and with either a mandolin or a peeler, shave the asparagus stalks across the diagonal.

Combine all ingredients in a large bowl. Squeeze the leftover membrane and any juice of the orange on top of the greens, toss gently with your hands, and sprinkle with asparagus tips. Serve immediately.

Pesto Roasted Asparagus

Cooking times will vary with width of the asparagus. Serves 4 to 6

2 pounds asparagus, ends cut or snapped off; about 2 bunches
3 tablespoons pesto
2 teaspoons extra virgin olive oil
2 teaspoons balsamic vinegar
1/4 teaspoon kosher salt
several grinds fresh black pepper

Preheat oven to 425 degrees. Combine everything but the asparagus in a small bowl. Place asparagus onto a shallow-sided roasting pan and pour the vinaigrette over the asparagus. Roast for 13 to 17 minutes or until the asparagus is tender but still bright green. Serve immediately.

FRIENDS & NEIGHBORS
Oysters Then and Now

This year the *Riggin* celebrates the 85th anniversary of her launching as an oyster dredger in 1927 on the Maurice River in Dorchester, New Jersey. One of the many in the *Riggin* fleet, Charles Riggin, a fisherman, had her built and named her after his two sons Jacob and Edward. She gained a fine reputation on the Delaware Bay as an able sailor, winning the only Oyster Schooner Race ever held in 1929. Although she doesn't dredge for oysters any longer, in honor of her history and to celebrate every week, we serve oysters from the Pemaquid Oyster Company located in Damariscotta, Maine just down the bay a bit from our homeport in Rockland.

Pemaquid Oyster Company was founded over 25 years ago along the Damariscotta River, a place that has oysters steeped in its shores and history. Evidence that oysters were part of the Native American diet over 1,000 years ago, the Glidden Midden, located on the shores of the river, is a huge ancient pile of oyster shells and the largest north of Georgia. Jeff (Smoky) McKeen, part of Pemaquid Oyster Company, delivers oysters to us, 120 per burlap bag, which then become appetizers for the first dinner on board each trip.

Oysters, like wine, carry the specific tastes of the place where they are grown, sometimes called 'merroir,' making the connection to the more commonly used word 'terroir' typically referring to wine production. However fancy you get with the language, the fact is that oysters from different areas have different flavors even if they are the same species. Pemaquid Oyster Company, like most oyster growers from Texas to New Brunswick, grows *Crassostrea virginica* more commonly known as either Eastern or American oysters.

You may have heard the old adage to never eat oysters during the months without 'r' in their name (which would mean from May to August). This may have been true years ago, but not so now. When oysters were first harvested on the *Riggin* in the 1920's and 30's, on-board refrigeration wasn't what it is today. The *Riggin*, a second-generation-style oyster-dredger, was built for speed, to get her daily catch back to the dock as soon as possible. This was because the fishing vessel that returned to dock first earned the best price; also, the fastest boat had the freshest oysters that spent the least amount of time in the warm summer temperatures. Now, we are lucky enough to have oysters plucked from the sea and chilled immediately. In addition, oysters spawn in water temperatures of 70 degrees or higher. Spawning tends to give a different (some say unpleasant) flavor to oysters and for several weeks after spawning, having expended all of their energy for reproductive pursuits, they have little substance to them. As anyone who has had the bracing opportunity to swim in Maine water knows, rarely and only in specific harbors does the temperature climb that high, so they don't typically spawn here, but instead are grown from 'seed', tiny oysters 2mm in size. What all this means in a nutshell (or oyster shell) is that we are free to eat oysters all summer long here in Maine!

Because oysters are so delicate in flavor and so nuanced in how they express their particular growing environment, I don't tend to serve them with much adornment. The French way is to have them with some lemon wedges, a baguette (or rye bread), really good butter and some sea salt. Sometimes I'll make a mignonette, a jazzy cocktail sauce or bake them with a roasted shallot breading, but most of the time I love to serve (and eat!) them without anything at all to really savor their individuality.

Oysters Mignonette

A classic and elegant way to serve oysters. To stabilize the oysters in their shells when serving, place them on either crushed ice, salt or a bed of seaweed. Plan on serving 3 to 4 well-scrubbed oysters per person if serving as an appetizer.

Oyster Shucking

Oysters are not only delicious; they are also the source of that satisfying moment of triumph when their shell is breached and you are able to get to the meat inside. To open an oyster you will need some protective gear, such as a rubber or other sturdy glove; not to protect you from the oyster itself, but from the knife that you hold should it slip. The rubber glove is for your non-dominant hand (that would be the hand holding the shell). I've seen more than one New Year's Eve celebration result in stitches so don't skip the glove. The other necessary tool is an oyster knife with a sturdy handle. These knives do not have sharpened edges or points, but are instead built for strength.

Wrap the oyster in a towel with the hinge facing out. Put your gloved hand over the toweled oyster and place the knife close to the hinge. Press firmly and wiggle until the oyster releases its muscle just a little and slide the knife in further to fully release the hinge. Then run the knife along the inside of the top and bottom shells to release the muscles connecting the oyster to the shell.

Mignonette Sauce

If you happen to have leftover sauce, drizzle it with olive oil over greens for a light, refreshing dressing..
Makes 1 cup

1/2 cup red wine vinegar
1/4 cup lemon juice; about 1 lemon
1/4 cup orange juice; about 1/2 an orange
2 tablespoons minced shallots; about 1 small shallot
1/2 teaspoon sea salt
2 tablespoons peppercorns, (preferably) red and/or green, toasted and crushed
2 tablespoons minced fresh chives (for garnish)

To toast the peppercorns, heat in a small skillet over medium heat until aromatic, stirring occasionally, about 5 minutes. Remove from the pan to a cutting board to cool and crush with either the bottom of a clean skillet or a meat mallet.

Combine vinegar, juices, shallots, salt and pepper in a small bowl. Set aside until ready to serve. Strain the sauce and use a tiny spoon to drizzle on the oysters at the last minute.

To serve
Shuck the oysters. While retaining the oyster and liquor (oyster juice) still in the bottom half of the oyster shell, place the oysters (in the half-shell) on the bed of your choice (salt, seaweed, or ice). You can cover and refrigerate for a brief time until ready to serve or serve immediately with the mignonette sauce drizzled on top and garnished with the minced chives.

July

When the air is hot and filled with moisture even late into the day, the last thing I want to do is head into the galley to create **more** heat. Maybe that's why cucumbers were created. Cool and delicious and mild enough to lend themselves to innumerable combinations, we usually have our first sightings of home-grown cukes in the garden at the end of July. Luckily, there is no end to what can be done with these mild herbal-tasting vegetable because once they begin to emerge, there seems to be no stopping them.

LET'S GROW
Harvesting Memories & Enchantment in Our Garden

When I was a little girl, my brothers and I would go to my grandparent's house in rural New York for three weeks every summer. Our time was spent driving around with Grandpa in absolute delight on his John Deere riding mower; or helping Grandma in the garden and then canning what we'd harvested. I didn't think much about it then; save those John Deere pinnacles, while we weren't bored, we never found it all that exciting either. I find it poignant that I now often catch myself thinking of my Grandma and those memories when I'm in my own garden, either by myself or with my girls. The feeling is fills my heart – and is one of the reasons that I garden.

The memories of gardening enchant me. Watching seeds grow into healthy, strong plants that fairly burst out of the garden is delightful and good for my soul. Watching the girls watch the garden is equally delightful. Walking through the garden hand in hand with the girls and greeting my old friends, the perennials, and new friends, the annuals (including the vegetables) is peaceful and relaxing. The beauty that these friends give to our yard is rejuvenating. THIS is why I garden.

I also garden for the exercise and the healthy food, but frankly there are easier (and less hot and sticky) ways to achieve both. I've heard that fruits and vegetables are routinely sold at what's called a "farmer's market", so why on earth would I choose to grow my own? It may save me money; but honestly, I've never figured if what I spend on the four to five yards of compost, seed, tools, grow lights, electricity and water actually "saves" me money.

But truly, there isn't a taste that is better on this planet than a sun-warmed tomato eaten right off the vine. Or asparagus that's been just picked, run straight back to the house, and plunked into boiling water. Or sweet corn that we've managed to harvest before the raccoons (and winning against the raccoons always adds a distinct taste of success and a dash of satisfaction to the flavor).

I wonder how the gardens will enchant me this summer? What volunteers will show themselves as unexpected guests? What vegetable will become the Olympian grower this year? Maybe I'll wander through the garden in the early morning when the dew is still clinging to the leaves and enjoy my morning coffee. Maybe I'll create spaces within that entice me to pause and sit. Perhaps a little arch made out of bent wood to welcome us at the entrance or a small bench made of stones and a board, or a tall trellis that blocks our view of the entire garden and beckons us to see what's beyond it.

The memories I have of gardening are rich and warm, beginning with my grandmother and still being created with our girls. So thank you Grandma, for the gift of gardening that you passed down to me – and for the time that you still spend in the garden with me and the girls. For when I'm out there, I always feel you with me.

Cucumber and Roasted Corn Salsa on Grilled Bread with Goat Cheese

This salsa is excellent with either blanched or grilled corn. If you are using the grill for another dish, place 3 ears of unhusked corn over medium-high heat and grill for 8 to 10 minutes, turning to cook all sides. If the grill isn't handy, blanching is the easier method.

Serve this salsa with the grilled bread (below) for a hearty appetizer or atop some greens for a light dinner. Makes about 2 cups

1 1/2 cups corn kernels; about 3 ears of corn
2 cups seeded and finely diced cucumber; about 1 medium cucumber
1/4 cup minced red onion
1 1/2 cups finely diced tomatoes; about one medium tomato
3 tablespoons lime juice; about one lime
2 tablespoons extra virgin olive oil
1/4 teaspoon salt
several grinds fresh black pepper

Bring a small pot of salted water to boil. Add the corn to the pot and cook for 1 minute. Drain corn immediately, reserving liquid for soup in another meal and remove the kernels from the cobs. Discard the cobs. Combine all ingredients in a medium-sized bowl. Can be made up to 1 hour ahead.

Grilled Bread

This bread is wonderful with or without the goat cheese and/or as a side for soup or grilled meats and is one of my favorite ways to use day old bread. Makes 12 to 15 slices

1 baguette or other rustic bread
1/2 cup extra virgin olive oil
1/2 cup crumbled goat cheese
kosher salt
several grinds fresh black pepper

Slice baguette on the diagonal into 3/4 to 1-inch slices. Use a pastry brush to coat both sides of the bread with olive oil and place onto a medium-high grill. Grill 1 to 2 minutes. On the second side, sprinkle each slice with salt, pepper and goat cheese. Cover the grill and cook another 1 to 2 minutes. Serve with the Avocado and Cucumber Gazpacho (page 81), or top with the Cucumber and Roasted Corn Salsa, above.

Avocado and Cucumber Gazpacho

On the Riggin *I need to use a potato masher to make this soup as the electrical cord that "plugs in the blender" doesn't reach all the way to shore. You, however, have the distinct advantage of a short distance from blender to plug.* Serves 4

3 avocados, pitted and peeled
2 tablespoons fresh mint
1/4 cup fresh whole basil leaves
2 teaspoons mashed garlic; about 1 large clove
2 tablespoons lemon juice; about 1/2 a lemon
1/2 cup lime juice; about 3 limes
4 cups vegetable or chicken broth
3 cucumbers, peeled, seeded and coarsely chopped
1/2 teaspoon salt
several grinds fresh black pepper

Combine all ingredients in a blender and pulse until fully blended. Season to taste with salt and pepper. Chill for at least an hour or overnight and serve cold.

Cucumber, Udon and Toasted Sesame Salad

Serves 4

1 (12.8-ounce) package udon noodles
1 1/2 English (seedless) cucumbers, sliced into thin half-rounds
1 cup minced scallions; about 1 bunch
1/2 red bell pepper, cored, seeded and julienned; about 1 cup
1 tablespoon black sesame seeds
2 tablespoons toasted sesame oil
3 tablespoons soy sauce
1 tablespoon lime juice; about 1/2 a lime

Cook the udon noodles according to package instructions. Rinse briefly with cool water and drain well. Combine all ingredients in a medium-sized bowl. Toss gently and serve immediately

August

For some, our lobster bakes are the highlight of the trip, when we go ashore on an uninhabited island and spend half a day preparing and then feasting on a traditional Maine lobster bake with all the trimmings. For me, it's a chance to hang with guests, sit in the shade, read with the girls, hold hands with Jon and look out on the gorgeous bay that is our home for the summer. We've even been known to take up a game or two of marshmallow tennis or baked potato baseball.

Lobster and Spinach Salad with a Lime and Chive Aioli

Note that cooking times will increase when cooking hard shell lobster to about 10 minutes per pound.
Serves 2

8 ounces cooked lobster meat; about 2, 1 1/4-pound lobsters
1 cup diced tomatoes; about 1 small tomato
1/4 cup Lime and Chive Aioli (see below)
1/8 teaspoon salt
several grinds fresh black pepper

Lobster Salad
To cook lobster, bring 1-inch of salted water to boil over high heat. Add the lobsters and cover. Cook for 8 to 10 minutes or until the entire shell is red and the antennae pull off easily. Remove from the pot and set aside to cool in a large bowl. Save the liquid for a future bisque or soup. When the lobsters are cooled, remove the meat from the claw and tail shells. Discard the vein that runs down the back of the tail and then coarsely cut the lobster meat. Combine with the rest of the lobster salad ingredients and serve on top of the dressed spinach.

Spinach
3 ounces baby spinach, washed and drained well; about 4 cups lightly packed
2 tablespoons extra virgin olive oil
2 teaspoons lime juice; about 1/2 a lime
1/8 teaspoon salt
several grinds fresh black pepper

Place the spinach in a medium sized bowl and add the rest of the ingredients. Toss and divide evenly onto two serving plates.

Lime and Chive Aioli

Makes a little over 1/2 cup

1 small clove garlic, smashed and coarsely chopped
1 tablespoon minced chives, plus a little extra for garnish
1 egg yolk
1 teaspoon Dijon mustard
2 teaspoons lime juice
dash of Worcestershire

1/8 teaspoon salt
several grinds fresh black pepper
2 tablespoons extra virgin olive oil
1/2 cup canola oil

Combine all ingredients except oils in a food processor and pulse until combined. Ever so slowly, while the motor is running, add the oil. After about a minute of dribbling the oil in, you can add it more quickly. Refrigerate for up to two days.

Lobster and Avocado Dip/Salad

Serve as either a dip with crackers or nested on a bed of greens as a salad. Either is an interesting way to serve our highly prized Maine delicacy. Makes 1 1/2 cups

6 ounces picked lobster meat, finely diced; about 2, 1-pound lobsters
1 avocado, peeled and diced; about 1 cup
2 tablespoons lime juice; about 1/2 a lime
1 tablespoon extra virgin olive oil
2 to 3 dashes of Worcestershire
2 tablespoons minced fresh basil
pinch of salt
several grinds fresh black pepper

Combine all ingredients and serve immediately.

On our Lighthouses and Lobsters Trips, we make sure to buy extra lobster so I can serve it at least three times in different permutations on the trip and these are two of the many ways we enjoy it. Of course there's always a non-lobster-lovers option as well!

Salad with Kalamata Olives, Feta and Mint

If you like to work ahead, you can mix the dressing ahead of time and then combine it with the rest of the ingredients when you are ready to serve. Serves 4 to 6

4 cups mixed greens or mesclun mix
1 1/2 cups sliced endive leaves, about 1 endive
1 1/2 cups romaine lettuce, coarsely chopped, about 2 to 3 large romaine lettuce leaves
1/4 cup Kalamata olives in oil, pitted and halved
2 ounces Feta cheese, crumbled; about 1/2 cup
1 cup cherry tomatoes, halved

Dressing:
3 tablespoons extra virgin olive oil
1/4 cup lightly packed mint leaves, julienned
1/4 cup orange juice, about 1/2 an orange
1 tablespoon lemon juice
1/8 teaspoon salt
1/8 teaspoon freshly ground black pepper

Mix all ingredients together and serve.

Spinach, Green Bean and Corn Salad with Blue Cheese Dressing

Grilled steak or chicken breasts would be a nice accompaniment to this salad to make a more filling meal. Serve with savory scones or Grilled Bread (page 80) without the goat cheese. Serves 4

6 ounces spinach greens; about 8 cups
1/2 cup thinly sliced red onion
8 ounces green beans, stems ends removed and cut in half or thirds; about two large handfuls,
2 cups fresh corn; about 4 ears
1/2 teaspoon kosher salt
several grinds fresh black pepper
2 tablespoons extra virgin olive oil
2 tablespoons lime juice; about 1/2 a lime
4 generous tablespoons Creamy Blue Cheese Dressing (page 87)

Build salads on 4 plates by dividing the spinach evenly between the plates. Top each salad with an equal portion of all ingredients.

Creamy Blue Cheese Dressing

This can be refrigerated for several days – it only gets better.. Makes 1 cup

2 1/2 ounces blue cheese, crumbled
5 tablespoons buttermilk
3 tablespoons sour cream
2 tablespoons mayonnaise
2 teaspoons white wine vinegar
1/4 teaspoon sugar
1 teaspoon minced garlic; about 1 clove
1/8 teaspoon salt
1/8 teaspoon fresh pepper
dash of Worcestershire

Whisk all the ingredients together and refrigerate until ready to serve.

Creative Kitchen

Tools For Inspired Cooks

Most recipes do not stand on their own, but are enhanced by the other dishes with which they are combined. Those who need exact recipes to do their cooking work should simply enjoy this window into a different way of thinking about how recipes can connect with each other. Those who wish to explore - have at it and don't stop here!

Handkerchief Pasta	*with* Chicken, Basil & Sun-dried Tomato Sausage + Spinach + Peppers + Cream	*with* Chili-Rubbed Pot Roast + Onions + Cream	*in* Cream Of Mushroom Soup, Asian Style
Chili-Rubbed Pot Roast	*with* Blue Cheese Dipping Sauce	*in* A Sandwich With Sourdough Bread	*with* Spinach, Green Bean & Corn Salad
Thai-Inspired Maine Shrimp Cakes	*with* Cucumber & Roasted Corn Salsa	*with* Yogurt & Chive Sauce	*with* Chive &Tomato Garnish
Pan-Fried Monkfish	*with* Yogurt & Chive Sauce	*with* Black Bean, Avocado And Goat Cheese Salad	*with* Chive & Tomato Garnish
Melted Gouda, Artichoke & Spinach	*in* An Omelet	*on* A Pizza	*with* Handkerchief Pasta
Broccoli With Roasted Red Onion	*in* Chicken Pot Pie (In place of asparagus)	*with* Crispy Pasta	*with* Creamy Lemon Over Whole Wheat Penne
Pesto Roasted Asparagus	*in* An Omelet	*on* A Pizza	*with* Handkerchief Pasta
Lobster & Spinach Salad	*on* A Pizza	*on* An Omelet	*with* Ricotta Gnocchi
Mignonette Sauce	*as* Dressing For Kale Salad		

Lime & Chive Aioli	*on* Pan-Fried Monkfish or Seared Scallops	*on* Thai-Inspired Maine Shrimp Cakess	
Lobster And Avocado Dip/Salad	*with* Whole Wedged Tomato	*on* Sourdough Bread + Havarti + Tomato Slices	
Spinach, Green Bean & Corn Salsa	*with* Ricotta Gnocchi	*with* Handkerchief Pasta	
Risotto	*with* Chili-Rubbed Pot Roast	*with* Broccoli + Roasted Red Onion	
Root Vegetable & Mushroom Soup	*with* Ricotta Gnocchi	*in* Baked Gnocchi With Garlic & Cream	
Spinach And Lime Confetti Salad	*with* Pan-Fried Monkfish	*with* Hummus & Parsley Rice Cakes	*with* Seared Scallops
Hummus And Parsley Rice Cakes	*with* Chive & Tomato Garnish	*with* Cucumber & Roasted Corn Salsa	
Potato Cilantro Waffles	*with* Poached Egg + Lobster & Avocado Dip/Salad	*with* Creamy Stilton Dressing + Kale Salad + Chili-Rubbed Pot Roast	
Roasted Carrots, Red Onion & Kale	*in* Baked Gnocchi With Garlic & Cream		
Chicken, Basil And Sun-dried Tomato Sausage	*with* Kale Salad + Handkerchief Pasta		
Cucumber, Udon And Toasted Sesame Salad	*with* Spicy Green Beans & Orange Bell Peppers		
Cucumber And Roasted Corn Salsa	*with* Pan-Fried Monkfish Seared Scallops		
Granola	*in* Sourdough Bread		

September

Wood stoves are hot, and the black box of wood-heated iron is what I use to make meals for 30 people all summer long. But all stoves, and therefore all kitchens, are hot. Doesn't matter if you are standing in a restaurant kitchen or in MY restaurant kitchen – the galley. However, when the breezes stiffen and the air freshens with the clear northwest breezes of fall, my galley is **the** place to come for a warm cup of tea – to warm not just your belly, but your hands! Plus there's nothing better than an apple crisp or a carrot-banana cake fresh from a wood stove.

COOKING WITH MY GIRLS
Mama, What's for Dinner?

It's the ever present question asked around the country at the roughly 5 o'clock hour when snack time is long gone and dinner time seems an age away. Sometimes I have a ready answer as I'm already cooking away or I've been cooking all day testing and sorting recipes.

Other days, however, I have the same question myself. What IS for dinner? So I ask the girls – What do you want? What should we have?

Sometimes their after school days are filled to the brim, requiring that I've already planned ahead and can walk in the door and get dinner on the table in 20 minutes or less. Some days are more leisurely and the question, "What's for dinner?" can be a conversation and a process in which the girls are involved and are making up a recipe as we go along. I write down what we do so that we can re-create it.

The best part of this conversation is that it's teaching the girls to create on their own so that they have the choice to either follow a recipe or the creativity and confidence to make a meal without one.

While the setting is different, the process is not, as a similar conversation happens every morning in the galley when we are deciding what we will prep and make for the day's meals. The freshness of the produce, the weather and the schedule for the day all inform what it is we will make. While some would find it stressful not to know exactly what the menu is for the week before hand, I actually find it fun and freeing.

Recently, I splurged at a local Italian market in Portland called Micucci's so when the question of dinner came up that day, we had all sorts of choices from which to create. In general, shopping is not a favorite pastime of mine until I find myself in a specialty food store or farmer's market and then it's a completely different story. I came home with a box full of, among other things, broccoli raab, basil, tomatoes, prosciutto, Toscana salami, Parmigiano-Reggiano cheese, 12 year old balsamic vinegar, imported extra virgin olive oil, fresh ciabatta bread, and some assorted unusual pastas.

As I walked the box of amazing goodies into the kitchen, the fragrance of the basil filled the kitchen and we all immediately began touching and smelling and cooing over the produce and the shapes of the unusual pasta – already planning. Chlöe, our eldest, picked out the capunti pasta, shaped like an open canoe or peapod - appropriate of course. She loves the taste of basil and tomatoes together so the fresh, bushy Genovese basil had to be a part of our meal as did the perfectly ripe, small bright red tomatoes. The thinly sliced prosciutto was the next choice and then it was a natural to add the Parmesan.

Then the question of when to add what… Chlöe wanted to see the bright green of the basil, so that had to go in the skillet absolutely last or the heat from the pasta would turn it green brown instantly. The tomatoes could have been roasted, but she wanted the bright taste of them fresh, so they only go into the pan to just heat them through, not cook them.

Prosciutto, Tomato and Basil Capunti
We had this pasta with a simple salad of greens tossed with the silky 12 year old balsamic vinegar, the imported olive oil, sea salt and pepper. Serves 4 to 6

1 pound capunti pasta or other pasta such as penne or ziti
3 tablespoons extra virgin olive oil
1 pound fresh tomatoes, cored and cut into 1-inch chunks
1/4 teaspoon kosher salt
Several grinds of fresh black pepper
1/4 pound very thinly sliced prosciutto
1/2 cup lightly packed basil leaves
3 ounces freshly grated Parmigiano-Reggiano; about 1 cup

Bring a large pot of salted water to boil and following the cooking times on the pasta package cook the pasta al dente. When the pasta is nearly done, heat a large skillet over medium-high heat and add the oil. Carefully add the tomatoes and stir several times to heat, but not cook through. You want the tomatoes to maintain their shape. Sprinkle with salt and pepper. Remove pan from heat and lay the prosciutto slices on top of the tomatoes. Drain pasta. Add pasta to the skillet and then scatter basil leaves and Parmesan on top. Toss all together and serve immediately.

Apple Crisp with Pecan Topping

Of course you won't be able to resist serving this with vanilla ice cream. This is such a homey recipe and one of my dependable favorites. So when it was pouring down rain, freezing cold and we were hauled out this spring, I brought a warm pan down for the crew with a pot of tea. They all sat around the wood stove warming themselves with bowls of apple crisp and hot mugs of tea. Makes 15 servings

Filling
3 pounds tart apples; about 9 to 12 apples
1 tablespoon plus 1 teaspoon lemon juice
1 cup sugar
1/2 teaspoon ground cloves
1 teaspoon ground cinnamon

Topping
1 cup (2 sticks) unsalted butter
2 1/4 cups all-purpose flour
1 1/2 cups sugar
1/4 teaspoon salt
1 cup chopped pecans

Preheat oven to 400 degrees. Peel, core, and slice the apples into 1/4-inch wedges and toss them with the lemon juice. In a small bowl, combine the sugar and spices and sprinkle over the apples. Spread the apples evenly in an ungreased 9 x 13-inch pan. In a separate bowl, cut the butter into the flour until the mixture is coarsely blended. Mix the sugar, salt and pecans into the topping; mixture should be crumbly.

Place the topping on top of the apple mixture and bake for 45 minutes or until the top is browned and the liquid in the apples is dark.

Raspberry Cinnamon Galette

We have in our garden what is becoming a raspberry forest, where eventually the saddest thing happens and we get tired of eating raspberries. Even as I write this I find it tremendously unbelievable, but it's actually true. When this implausible moment occurs, we pick but don't eat them and freeze the berries for the middle of winter when we can't remember what it's like to be tired of eating raspberries. When using frozen berries in the galette, I bake it for 70 to 80 minutes. Serves 8

2 cups raspberries
1/4 cup sugar

1 tablespoon all-purpose flour
1/2 teaspoon ground cinnamon
1 tablespoon unsalted butter
1 tablespoon milk
1 tablespoon large grain sugar such as demerara or turbinado
1 galette crust

Preheat oven to 350 degrees. Line a baking sheet with parchment paper and place the galette crust onto the sheet. In a medium bowl, combine raspberries, sugar, flour and cinnamon. Toss together and place in the middle of the galette dough leaving a 2 to 3-inch border. Fold the border up and let the pleats fall naturally. Pinch them together where they fold. Dot the raspberries with little bits of the unsalted butter. Brush the edges of the dough with the milk and sprinkle with the large grain sugar. Bake for 30 to 35 minutes or until the raspberry center is bubbly and set up some the crust is golden brown. Serve warm or cool, cutting with a pizza wheel or sharp knife.

Galette Crust

This crust is a rustic one made so by the addition of the cornmeal. It is not as flaky as you think of a perfect pie crust, but is instead supported by the structure that the cornmeal provides. Makes enough for 2, 8-inch galettes

2 cups all-purpose flour
3/4 teaspoon salt
1 tablespoon sugar
1/4 cup cornmeal
1/2 cup (1 stick) chilled unsalted butter, cut into 1/2-inch cubes
1/2 cup ice water
1/4 cup buttermilk

Combine all of the dry ingredients. Add the butter and either press with your thumbs or use a pastry knife to incorporate. The mixture should look something between bread crumbs and small peas. The smaller the pieces, the more tender and flakier the crust. Add the ice water and buttermilk. If you need more liquid, add 1 teaspoon at a time until the mixture forms a ball. Divide into 2, cover well and put in freezer for 30 minutes. Lightly flour the counter top and roll out 1 disc into an 11-inch circle to receive the raspberry filling. Reserve 1 disc for another galette.

Millet Rum Raisin Muffins

Because I make my own vanilla, I'll sometimes use homemade bourbon vanilla in place of the rum and vanilla in the recipe.

On the boat I'm often cooking for folks who are gluten-free; even oatmeal (unless specifically labeled) is verboten, so for breakfast on the day I serve oatmeal, I'll make my gluten-free passengers either grits or millet with butter and then have extra for these muffins another morning. Millet is one of the ancient grains so important to early civilizations; nowadays it's making a comeback in the U.S. Millet has a nutty, corn-like flavor which works well as a side dish or in breads and pastries. These are the favored muffins for Toni, my assistant cook of five years, and she asks me to make them every week. Mmmmm. They are delicious. Gluten-free baking mix is easily substituted for the all-purpose flour in this recipe. Makes 1 dozen

2/3 cup raisins
1/3 cup rum
2 tablespoons vanilla extract
1 cup water
1/3 cup millet
2 cups all-purpose flour
1/2 teaspoon salt, plus a pinch of salt for the millet
1/2 teaspoon baking soda
1/2 teaspoon ground cinnamon
pinch ground cardamom
3/4 cup vegetable oil
1 cup sugar
1 large egg
2 small apples, peeled, cored, and roughly chopped

Soak the raisins in the rum and vanilla for at least 1 hour, or as long as overnight. Bring the water to a simmer in a small pan. Add the millet and a pinch of salt. Cover and simmer for 15 minutes then remove from heat and let rest for 10 minutes.

Preheat oven to 350 degrees. Grease muffin tins or use muffin liners. In a large bowl, mix together the dry ingredients. Add the oil, sugar, egg, and vanilla. Mix until just incorporated into the dry ingredients. Stir in the apples, raisins and millet. The batter is thicker than most. Fill muffin cups with the batter.

Bake about 25 to 35 minutes or until the muffins spring back when lightly pressed. Let rest in the tins for 5 minutes and then remove to cool the rest of the way.

Lemon Madeleine's

The initial recipe comes from Dorie Greenspan, my hero, in "Baking with Julia". Makes 24 cookies

3 tablespoons unsalted butter, melted, plus a little extra for the madeleine pan
1 1/4 cups sifted cake flour
1/8 teaspoon salt
2/3 cup sugar
2 eggs, room temperature
1 teaspoon vanilla extract
1 teaspoon lemon extract
2 teaspoons lemon zest; about 1 lemon

Preheat oven to 400 degrees. Butter 12-cookie madeleine pan generously. Sift the flour and 1 tablespoon of sugar onto parchment paper or waxed paper and set aside. Combine the sugar and eggs in a mixing bowl and immediately begin to whisk with either the whisk attachment or a hand-held mixer until the color has lightened considerably; the volume has tripled and the mixer forms ribbons on the surface for 10 seconds or so. Add vanilla extract, lemon extract and lemon zest and whisk briefly. Remove the bowl from the mixer and fold in the sifted flour and sugar in thirds. Add a little bit of the batter to the melted butter and gently fold, then fold the butter mixture into the rest of the batter in the mixing bowl. Do this ever so gently. Immediately spoon half of the batter into prepared pan. Bake for 5 to 6 minutes or until the cookies are spongy in the middle. Remove from pan and set on a cooling rack. Wipe the cookie pan clean, butter again generously, spoon rest of batter into the forms and bake again for 5 to 6 minutes.

Carrot-Banana Cake

This recipe was first printed in "At Home, At Sea". I've begun making it in a completely different and fancier way and thought that it deserved a reprint. Serves 12-16

Cake
2 cups all-purpose flour
1 tablespoon ground cinnamon
2 teaspoons baking soda
1/4 teaspoon salt
4 large eggs
1 cup vegetable oil
1 cup sugar
1 cup lightly packed light brown sugar
1 1/2 cups finely grated carrots; about 3 carrots
1 cup drained crushed pineapple in juice
1/2 cup mashed ripe banana; about 1 banana

Frosting
1 (8-ounce) package cream cheese, room temperature
1 cup powdered sugar
3 tablespoons unsalted butter, room temperature
1/4 teaspoon ground cinnamon
Additional ground cinnamon for garnish
1/2 cup toasted unsweetened coconut

Cake
Preheat oven to 350 degrees. Grease and flour two 9-inch round pans. Sift the first four ingredients into a medium bowl. In a large bowl, whisk the eggs, then whisk in the oil, sugar and brown sugar until well blended. Stir in the flour mixture. Add the carrots, pineapple, banana and blend well. Transfer the batter to the prepared pans. Bake until a tester inserted near the center of the cake comes out clean, about 40 to 45 minutes. Leave the cakes in the pans on a cooling rack for 10 minutes, then remove from the pans and cool completely.

Frosting
Beat all ingredients in a medium bowl until smooth and the consistency is just the teeniest bit runny. Lay one cake on a platter and frost just the top allowing the frosting to flow over the edges slightly. Place the second cake over the first and do the same with the frosting. Sprinkle with toasted coconut to finish.

October

Time to don cozy wool sweaters with high collars and pull out the felted fingerless gloves to keep ourselves warm as the days become shorter and the temperatures lower. The kerosene deck lanterns emerge early in the evening and are extinguished late in the morning gloam, lighting our faces in a warm glow. The other schooners have their deck lanterns and anchor light set as well; from a distance their soft lights beckon. But we are snug on the *Riggin* and gather in the galley to sing and listen to music from Capt's guitar.

AROUND THE TABLE
Eating Together

In the same way that the kitchen is the hub of the house, the table is really the hub of the kitchen; the place where we all gather. It's the place where we sit, breathe out, give thanks, look each other in the eye, share our days and our sustenance. Studies show that children, and especially teens, who eat with their families at the dinner table more than three times a week do better in school, eat healthier, have higher grades, delay having sex, are more active and less likely to smoke, drink, do drugs, get depressed, develop eating disorders and consider suicide. It's the closest thing we parents have to a magic wand.

For me, the dinner table (and I say 'dinner' but who really cares what meal your family connects over, only that you do connect) is at once a mundane, everyday event and a sacred rhythm that is emblematic of what we value – healthy food, family, relaxation….

Our modern world is a terrific one, with so many options and ways of living available to us. The realm of food in our family life is one of only a myriad of choices that we must make every day. While it's arguably freeing and delicious to have so many ways to shape our lives, the reverse is also true. Now that the restrictions on what a family looks like have been lifted (think the 1950's picture of mom at home making dinner and dad coming in the door at the end of the work day to set down his briefcase and join the family for the meal) the picture is now dependent on the choices we make.

While previous generations had the restriction of social norms, they also had the benefit of the rhythm created by those same norms. They also had practicality informing those rhythms. Before there were microwaves, frozen food, packaged food, and take-out food, there were wood stoves, no refrigeration and fewer ways of preserving food. When the food was done, you ate. Everyone ate at the same time because they had to. Now we need to be conscious enough, and aware enough, to create those rhythms and patterns for ourselves. Simply because we CAN eat meals anytime that is convenient to our schedules, doesn't mean that we aren't better off eating together and doing something more than just replacing calories and adding nutrition. Ritual, tradition, rhythm, habit life… it's up to us as leaders of our families to develop and maintain them - not only for our sanity, but also to engender a sense of unity and contentment in our lives.

There are several ways that we've found to help our family maintain the habit of eating dinner together:

• Everyone is involved. I usually cook, sometimes with help, sometimes not. The girls set the table, fold the napkins, light a candle, and arrange a flower or some other small center piece. Jon and the girls clean up.

• We say grace and give thanks for our day.

• The phone, TV and sometimes the radio are off.

• No one leaves the table until we are all finished eating.

• Everyone tells a story about their day. Sometimes it's a small one; sometimes it takes the whole meal. It can be funny, sad, poignant, infuriating or educational. Doesn't matter as long as we are sharing.

• If something is scheduled for one or more of us, we either eat together at a different time or dinner happens when most of us can eat.

Risotto with Roasted Root Vegetables

Serves 4 to 6

1/4 cup (1/2 stick) unsalted butter
1/2 cup minced onion; about 1 small onion
1/2 teaspoon kosher salt
2 cups Arborio rice
1 cup white wine
5 or 6 cups low-salt chicken or vegetable broth
3/4 cup grated Parmesan cheese
1 batch of Roasted Root Vegetables (recipe below)

In a medium saucepan, melt the butter over medium heat. Add the onions and salt and sauté until the onions are translucent, about 10 minutes. If the onions begin to brown, reduce heat. When the onions are done add the rice and stir with a wooden spoon for one minute. Add the white wine and stir. Bring the wine to a simmer, stirring occasionally. When the liquid has mostly evaporated, (which you can tell by sight of course, but you can also hear as the rice begins to crackle just a little). Add 1 cup of the chicken broth and stir until the liquid is (again) nearly completely absorbed. Continue to add the broth, one cup at a time, until it is all incorporated, stirring frequently and listening for changes in the sounds of the rice. The rice takes about 25 to 30 minutes to cook; it's done when the liquid is completely incorporated but everything is still creamy and the grains are just the tiniest bit al dente in the center. Stir in the Parmesan. Salt to taste. Serve immediately with Roasted Root Vegetables.

Roasted Root Vegetables

If you'd like to plan ahead for leftover root vegetables, double this recipe. You may need to increase the cooking time (or use two baking sheets). Serves 4 to 6

1 1/2 pounds onions; about 2 onions
1 pound carrots; about 4 large carrots
1 pound parsnips; about 3 large parsnips
1 1/2 pounds sweet potatoes; about 2 medium sweet potatoes
2 tablespoons olive oil
1/4 teaspoon salt
1/8 teaspoon freshly ground black pepper
16 ounces whole button mushrooms

Preheat oven to 400 degrees. Peel the onions, carrots, parsnips and sweet potatoes. Cut all vegetables into large 1 to 1 1/2-inch chunks. Toss with oil, salt, and pepper and place on a shallow baking sheet. Roast for 50 minutes then add the mushrooms. Roast for another 20 to 30 minutes or until all the vegetables are tender when pierced with a fork and beginning to brown on the edges.

Root Vegetable and Mushroom Soup

To puree this soup safely, work in batches, only filling the blender about two-thirds full. Be sure to leave the top open a bit in order to release the steam. Cover with a cloth before pulsing as gently as you can to start. Once it's going a little, you can leave the switch on and walk away, pureeing for a minute or two per batch. It should be very smooth without anything "curdley" or bumpy looking when it's done. Serves 4 to 6 easily

3 tablespoons extra virgin olive oil
3 cups diced onions; about 2 medium onions
5 cups Roasted Root Vegetables (page 106)
1 teaspoon salt
several grinds fresh black pepper
6 cups low-salt vegetable or chicken broth
2 tablespoons unsalted butter
5 ounces sliced button mushrooms; about 2 cups

In a large stockpot, heat the olive oil over medium-high heat. Add the onions and sauté until translucent, about 10 minutes. Add the cooked root vegetables, salt and pepper. Cook with the onions for a few minutes then add the broth and simmer for about 30 minutes.

While the onions and vegetables are simmering, sauté the mushrooms. In a medium skillet, melt the butter over medium heat. Add the mushrooms and a pinch of salt and pepper and sauté until the mushrooms are cooked through, about 5 to 7 minutes. Set aside.

Once the vegetables have finished simmering remove from heat and purée, being careful to leave an opening for pressure to escape. Purée each batch for at least 1 to 2 minutes before transferring back to the pot. Add the mushrooms, making sure that you scrape any good brown bits off the bottom of the skillet.

Roasted Carrots, Red Onion and Kale

Curly or Russian kale will get a little crispy on the edges in this recipe while Lacinato kale (the longer more wrinkled variety) will wilt more like other greens do. Both are delicious. Serves 4 to 6

1 1/2 pounds carrots, sliced into 1/4-inch slices; about 6 large carrots
1/2 red onion, sliced thinly
1/2 teaspoon kosher salt, plus another 1/4 teaspoon for the kale
several grinds fresh black pepper
2 tablespoons olive oil, plus another 2 tablespoons for the kale
6 ounces kale stemmed and coarsely chopped; about 1/2 a bunch

Preheat oven to 400 degrees. On a large roasting pan, drizzle olive oil and sprinkle salt and pepper over the carrots and onions. Use your hands to coat evenly. Roast for 40 minutes or until the carrots are tender and the onions are beginning to brown. Add the kale and drizzle with more oil, salt, and pepper. Stir well and roast for another 15 minutes or until the kale is bright green and a little crispy on the edges.

Pumpkin Ravioli with Prosciutto, Sage and Spinach

Once you've made your ravioli, you can freeze them for use at a later time. Place the uncooked raviolis on a floured sheet tray. Freeze for several hours then transfer to an air tight container and keep in the freezer until ready to use.

The secret for easy ravioli is to use wonton wrappers (which you'll find, refrigerated, in most grocery stores) as your pasta dough. If you would prefer to make your own dough, double the pasta recipe for Spicy Hand-kerchief Pasta Soup (page 17). Serves 4 to 6; makes 48 ravioli

Ravioli
1 3/4 cup cooked, pureed pumpkin or 1 (15-ounce) can pumpkin puree
1/2 cup grated Parmesan cheese
1 cup ricotta cheese
3 eggs
1/4 teaspoon freshly grated nutmeg
1/4 teaspoon salt
several grinds fresh black pepper
2 packages wonton wrappers, 48 per package

Sauce
4 ounces sliced prosciutto, cut into 1/2-inch strips
6 tablespoons unsalted butter

1/3 cup lightly packed sage leaves
1 pound spinach, deribbed, cleaned and dried

Garnish
1/2 cup grated Parmesan cheese

Ravioli
Combine all ingredients except wonton wrappers in medium-sized bowl. Bring a large
pot of salted water to boil. Lay 8 or 12 wonton wrappers out on a floured counter. Dot
each one with a tablespoon of filling. With a pastry brush, brush a thin layer of water
around the edges. Place another wrapper on top and with your fingers, press the edges flat
together. Repeat. When all of the ravioli are done, quickly add to the water and wait until
they float to the top, stirring at the beginning with a wooden spoon. When they float to
the top, they are done. Remove with a slotted spoon to the pan with the sauce. Toss gently
and serve immediately with grated Parmesan cheese.

Sauce
Heat a large skillet over medium-high heat. Add the butter, prosciutto and sage leaves.
Sauté until the butter begins to brown and add the spinach. Remove from heat and wait
for the ravioli to be done.

Carrots and Leeks au Gratin

If you grew leeks in your garden this year or belonged to a CSA, you must have, by now, a small mountain
of leeks. If not, they are a good deal because they're in season, and worth enjoying in abundance. Leeks
don't root cellar well – although I have found that if I leave them in the ground covered with a deep layer
of straw that I can pull them as I need them over the winter. Serves 4 to 6

1 tablespoon olive oil
4 cups carrots, peeled and cut into 1-inch pieces; about 2 large carrots
1/2 teaspoon salt
several grinds fresh black pepper
4 cups leeks, cleaned and chopped into 1-inch pieces; about 3 medium leeks
1 cup heavy cream

Preheat oven to 375 degrees. Heat a large skillet over medium-high heat. Add the oil, carrots, salt and pepper. Sauté for 10 to 15 minutes. Transfer to an oven safe casserole, add
the leeks and drizzle the cream over the top. Bake for 35 to 45 minutes or until the edges
are beginning to brown, the vegetables are tender and the cream has mostly evaporated.

LEFTOVERS DONE RIGHT
Pizza

I first started sailing as a mess cook twenty plus years ago; the difference between how I cooked then and how I cook now is as big as the world, and as small as an ice chest. When I began sailing as a mess cook we had, literally, an ice chest. At the beginning of a six-day trip, 600 pounds of ice would travel on the shoulders of two deckhands, down the ramp, up and over the rail and into the ice box, a deep, well-insulated wooden chest with a hinged lid. Then the week's worth of meat, dairy and vegetables would be tightly packed (like a well-planned vacation itinerary) into the ice, with Friday night's turkey on the bottom, Monday night's fish resting on the surface, and everything else sandwiched in between.

With only ice as refrigeration and few venues to buy additional ice (no grocery stores 5 minutes away when you're sailing!), it was crucial to avoid the inevitable ice loss that resulted from adding lukewarm leftover soup or other meals to the ice chest. Instead, we had a slop bucket into which all vegetable scraps, leftover soups and other meals would go. Very little was saved; but then very little remained of our carefully planned, routine meals. Our trips were all six days and we knew the day by the meal. Fish – Monday night; fish chowder – Tuesday lunch; turkey – Friday night. It might sound monotonous, but for those guests coming once or twice a year, it was something to look forward to (the "delight" in the food routine was another story for the crew). The set menu was also incredibly efficient in terms of prep and food costs.

Much has changed over the past twenty plus years. We have a battery operated refrigeration system which means the deckhands no longer lug 600 pounds of ice on board every week, but there's still plenty to schlep (just ask the crew!). The wood stove is still heated with, well, wood, so 18 crates need to be loaded every week. Then there are all the supplies that keep the *Riggin* happily sailing. And of course there is the food.

In the beginning, we had a standing order for the same items every week. Since then, my cooking has changed dramatically; this is partly because I have years of cooking experience to fall back on, but also because how I buy food has changed. Like the rest of the country, Maine is now brimming with seasonal vegetables and local purveyors of cheeses, meats, mushrooms… the list goes on and I take advantage of it all. This means that our menu is very different from week to week (save the favorites like Congo Bars!) and I rarely know exactly what I'm cooking until it arrives in my galley – boxes and assorted bags overflow with freshly-picked, colorful produce and all but obscure the galley tables while we oooh and aaah and then sort and store.

What this also means is that I end up with a lot more leftovers because it's much harder to gauge how much a group of 30 will eat when I'm making up the menu and recipes as I go along. I've become an expert at how to serve leftovers without making them seem like leftovers. The day after we have Salmon with Tri-Pepper Salsa, Spicy Roasted Lemon Kale and Caramelized Spring Onion Quinoa we do NOT have Salmon, Kale and Quinoa Soup for lunch. Instead, we might have Salmon Cakes with Lemon Aioli as an appetizer; Quinoa Honey Whole Wheat Bread with lunch; and Italian Sausage and Kale Soup another day. Or pizza….

Pizza is a perfect way to use up little bits that didn't find their way into bellies the first · time around. Small bits of cheese, one or two strips of crumbled bacon; roasted vegetables from a previous dinner; grilled chicken breast; almost anything is fair game. Indulge yourself in a little creativity while satisfying the part of you that likes to use up everything in the refrigerator.

The dough recipe will make one large or two small pizzas.
For one large pizza, the ratio for little bits of this and that in your fridge should be:

1 cup tomato sauce (if you like)
1/2 pound grated and/or crumbled cheese
1/2 pound meat such as sausage, prosciutto, bacon or salami
1/2 pound cooked vegetable such as asparagus, broccoli, broccoli raab, onions and/or peppers
OR
1/2 pound uncooked vegetables such as sliced tomato or spinach

Many people think of broccoli raab as too bitter. But when it's blanched, much of the bitterness leaches out and it becomes more acceptable to most palates, especially, as in this recipe, when balanced by the rich, salty taste of the sausage. Broccoli raab is a popular Italian vegetable and given that it's high in all vitamins and minerals related to leafy, green vegetables, it's worth a try.

If you don't have time to make the dough, you can usually find white or whole wheat pizza dough in the deli or prepared foods section of your grocery store refrigerated and ready to roll out.

So I've given you the basics, and some ideas for combining what you have. But I can't resist giving you my favorite pizza recipe, which I often make on the boat as a way of using up leftover broccoli raab and sausage.

Pizza with Italian Sausage, Broccoli Raab and Rosemary

This recipe, while it calls for broccoli raab, is perfect for most hearty greens, such as kale, swiss chard, turnip greens and beet greens. Blanching them and then sautéing them with the sausage sweetens them a little and also evaporates the excess water that makes pizza soggy. Serves 4

2 tablespoons olive oil
1 pound Italian sausage, spicy if you prefer, cut into 1/2-inch chunks
10 ounces broccoli raab, coarsely chopped; about 5 cups or 1 bunch
1 tablespoon minced fresh rosemary
Several grinds of fresh black pepper
1/4 teaspoon salt
2 tablespoons olive oil
1 pizza dough (page 113)

Preheat oven to 450 degrees. Place a pizza stone into the oven on the top shelf (if you don't have a pizza stone, use a baking sheet with the bottom side facing up.) Bring a medium pot of salted water to a boil. In a large skillet, heat the oil over medium-high heat. Add the sausage and cook until it begins to brown on the outside. When the sausage is nearly done and the water is boiling, add the broccoli raab to the pot of water. Blanch for 1 minute, then using a large slotted spoon or flat strainer, remove the broccoli raab from the water, allowing the broccoli raab to drain well. Transfer to the pan with the sausage. Add the rosemary, salt and pepper and mix well; continue cooking until any excess water has evaporated.

Dust the counter with flour and press or roll your pizza dough out to a little less than the diameter or width of the pizza stone or baking sheet. If you own a pizza peel, dust it now with corn meal. If not, dust the baking sheet. Transfer the dough to the pizza peel. Drizzle the dough with olive oil and spread the sausage and broccoli raab over the dough. To transfer the pizza to the stone, angle the peel and wiggle the peel assertively to encourage the pizza to slide off, removing the peel as you go.

Bake for 20 minutes or until the crust is golden brown on the bottom.

Pizza Dough

If you double this recipe, you can use the second batch to make focaccia or a loaf of crusty Italian bread for another meal. Makes dough for 1 large pizza

3/4 tablespoons yeast, or 1package
1 1/2 teaspoons salt
2 1/2 cups all-purpose flour
1 cup warm water
1 tablespoon olive oil
cornmeal for dusting

Combine the yeast, salt, and flour in a large bowl. Stir in all the remaining ingredients, reserving 1/4 cup water. Add more water if needed. Knead for 10 to 15 minutes by hand or 3 to 4 minutes with a dough hook. Oil the bowl and the top of the dough, cover, and set aside in a warm, draft free place to rise until doubled (about 1 hour).

November

Home now and the boat is put to bed for the season. I have to constantly remind myself that I'm only cooking for 4 people, not 30. The home oven heats twice as fast as the wood stove, so I also need a reminder to not turn it on at 3 P.M. in order to get dinner on the table by 6 P.M. The girls are both in school, we talk less, rest more. We read, nap, hike, nap, eat and nap again for at least a week; then we're ready to rejoin the world.

Spinach and Lime Confetti Salad

Makes 4 cups

4 ounces minced spinach; about 2 cups
2 cups peeled, seeded and diced cucumbers; about 1 cucumber
1 cup finely diced tomatoes, about 1 small tomato
2 tablespoons lime juice; about 1/2 a lime
1/4 teaspoon salt
2 tablespoons extra virgin olive oil
1 tablespoon red wine vinegar
1/4 teaspoon Worcestershire

Combine all ingredients in a medium sized bowl. Serve within 1 hour.

Roasted Whole Pumpkin

Pumpkin can be used as a wonderful vegetable for a meal or in pumpkin soup and other goodies. I've not given specific amounts for the ingredients as much of it depends on how big the pumpkin is. Taste first and then flavor..

1 small whole pumpkin
kosher salt and fresh black pepper
brown sugar and butter

Preheat oven to 400 degrees. Cut the pumpkin in half and remove the seeds and pulp. Place on a baking sheet flesh side down. Roast for 1 1/2 hours or until the center is tender. Scrape the flesh into a bowl and discard the skin. Sprinkle with salt, pepper and brown sugar and dot with butter. Mash the flesh with a potato masher. Serve immediately and freeze any leftover flesh in 16-ounce batches so that you can use them easily in future recipes.

Potato Spinach Salad with Lemon and Mustard

I love these potatoes with anything grilled. It's a perfect make-ahead dish and goes well with almost anything. Serves 4 to 6 generously

1 1/2 pounds Yukon Gold or other yellow, creamy potatoes, peeled; about 4 potatoes
2 tablespoons stone ground mustard

2 tablespoons lemon juice; about 1/2 a lemon
2 tablespoons extra virgin olive oil
1/2 teaspoon kosher salt
several grinds fresh black pepper
1/2 cup very thinly sliced red onion
1 ounce spinach; 2 cups lightly packed fresh spinach

In a large pot, cover the potatoes with salted water; simmer until tender when pierced with a fork, about 40 minutes. Drain and lay out on a baking sheet to cool. The potatoes will look a little flaky. No worries. When they are cool enough to touch but still warm, break them into 1-inch (or so) pieces. This is a rustic dish, so the pieces don't all have to be the same size.

In a small bowl combine the mustard, lemon juice, olive oil, salt and pepper. Combine the potatoes with the onions, spinach and dressing in a large serving bowl or platter. Serve warm or cold.

Hummus and Parsley Rice Cakes

Serves 4 to 6; makes about 12 cakes

2 cups cooked jasmine rice
1/4 cup extra virgin olive oil
1 (15.5-ounce) can garbanzo beans, drained
1 cup minced parsley
2 tablespoons tamari
1/4 cup tahini
2 cloves garlic, mashed
1 tablespoon lemon juice

Measure the rice into a medium sized bowl. Pulse all ingredients EXCEPT rice and oil in a food processor. Combine with rice and form into golf ball-sized balls and then press into patties. Heat a large skillet over medium-high heat and add half the oil to the pan. Place the patties carefully into the skillet and fry 3 to 4 minutes per side in 2 or 3 batches, adding a little more oil for each batch. Serve with Chive and Tomato Garnish (page 119).

Chive and Tomato Garnish

Makes 1 1/4 cups

1 cup plain yogurt or sour cream
1 tablespoon chopped chives
1/4 cup diced tomatoes
1/4 teaspoon salt
1 teaspoon lime juice
pinch cayenne pepper

Mix all ingredients together and serve.

Crispy Pasta

*This will also work with leftover dried pasta, but is terrific with homemade pasta. This is an intention-
ally loose recipe intended for the vagaries of the amount of leftover pasta with which you find yourself. The
amount of onions in this recipe is intended for 4 to 6 people, but if you want to increase or decrease the
amount of pasta, then do so accordingly with the onions.* Makes 1 cup

a handful of cold cooked pasta per person
1/2 tablespoon olive oil per person
1 cup caramelized onions (recipe below)
1 to 2 tablespoons grated Parmesan cheese per person
salt and black pepper to taste

Preheat oven to 375 degrees. Toss the pasta with olive oil in a roasting pan. Place pan
on middle shelf in oven. Bake until the edges crisp up and turns golden brown, 20 to 40
minutes. Toss with the rest of ingredients and bake for another 3 to 5 minutes. Serve immediately.

Caramelized Onions

1 tablespoon canola oil
3 cups sliced onions; about 2 medium onions

Heat a medium skillet over medium-high heat. Add the oil and then the onions. Cook the
onions until they are deep brown and very soft, about 20 to 30 minutes, reducing heat to
medium-low when the onions begin to brown on the bottom of the pan.

LEFTOVERS DONE RIGHT
Omelets

Passengers and friends often ask what I like to cook most. Bread is always my first answer; such simple ingredients, such complex reactions. But bread is a topic for another time. My second choice isn't a specific something to cook, but rather a way of cooking. I love to make dinner from nothing. And by 'nothing' I mean the sort of nothing embodied in the statement, "There's nothing to eat in this house/refrigerator/cupboard." The sort of 'nothing' that has my girls opening up the fridge and standing there cooling off the kitchen while they gaze unfocused into shelves full of mysterious and somehow unapproachable containers of leftovers. There's some of this, a little of that and not much of anything. The little bits of who-knows-what get arranged and rearranged in the refrigerator, but no one is brave enough to figure out how to use them.

I come from a family that was dedicated to using leftovers. My dad took leftovers seriously; he took them to work for lunch during the week and on the weekends, he and my brothers would raid the refrigerator. As the only girl in the family, I had to elbow my way in if I wanted to avoid the dregs. However, while my family honed its hockey-checking skills over leftovers, I have heard more than once from folks that leftovers are boring and "Who wants to have that again anyway?"

For me, leftovers are not about having the same meal again or even for the third time; I think of them as the building block, or a starting point, for an entirely different meal. Leftovers are actually a great way to boost flavor in subsequent meals because they already have flavor built into them. In the same way that soup or chili is even better on the second day, leftovers can be too.

This makes them perfect for use in a quick, weeknight meal of soup, frittata, pasta, quesadillas, pizza or omelets. It's also one of the hardest things to replicate in an actual recipe because we rarely have the same set of leftovers on any given day. That said, this segment is really more of a guide rather than scripture - a tool to help you use a basic recipe and adjust according to what you have on hand.

An omelet is a perfect breakfast meal of course, but it is also very good for dinner – full of protein, quick, elegant, European even. Add a warm baguette and a mixed greens salad dressed with good extra virgin olive oil and fresh lemon juice and you've an easy, nutritious meal in no time flat.

In this recipe I've given the amounts per omelet so that you could cook for a crowd or for one. While there are three variations on a cheese omelet listed here, the point is to use whatever small amounts of leftovers you have hanging around in the refrigerator - up to 4 ounces or 1/4 cup total of chopped ingredients per omelet. Also, it helps to heat the leftovers in a separate pan first so that you aren't cooking the eggs too long while waiting for the cold ingredients to heat up. Leftover roast beef? Make a beef and red onion omelet with feta. Leftover roast chicken? Make a chicken, tomato and scallion omelet. You get the idea. I like my omelets nice and cheesy, but if you prefer a little less, feel free to reduce the amount.

Mushroom, Potato and Cheddar Omelet
This omelet is perfect for leftover boiled or roasted potatoes from another meal. If you need to cook the pota-

toes for this meal, dice one red potato per omelet. Place in a pot of boiling salted water. Boil until potatoes are tender, about 5 to10 minutes. Drain and set aside. Makes 1 omelet

Filling:
1/2 tablespoon salted butter
1 ounce sliced button mushrooms; about 1 large mushroom
2 to 3 ounces diced, cooked potatoes; about 1/2 cup
1 ounce grated Cheddar cheese; about 1/2 cup lightly packed
pinch of salt and pepper

Omelet:
1/2 tablespoon salted butter
3 eggs
pinch of salt
several grinds of fresh black pepper

Filling
Melt 1/2 tablespoon butter in a small nonstick sauté pan over medium-high heat. Add the mushrooms and salt and pepper lightly. When the mushrooms are beginning to brown, add the potatoes and stir briefly just to heat the potatoes. If you've just boiled the potatoes, omit this step. Remove from the pan and set the filling aside in a small bowl. Carefully wipe the pan clean with a cloth or wash and then return to heat.

Omelet
Heat the pan on medium-high heat and add 1/2 tablespoon butter. Crack the eggs in a small bowl and whisk vigorously until they are well combined. Add the eggs to the pan as soon as the butter is melted and use a spatula to push the eggs to the center as you are moving the pan. When the eggs are almost done (they'll be firm but still shiny on top), add the cheese in the middle of the omelet in a straight line first, then the warm mushrooms and potatoes. With the spatula, fold 1/3 of the omelet over the filling. Shake the omelet to the far side of the pan and gently fold the omelet out of the pan, using your spatula and the edge of the pan to guide the omelet out of the pan and invert on a plate.

Asparagus, Tomato and Havarti Omelet
Makes 1 omelet

1/2 tablespoon salted butter
2 spears of asparagus cut into 1-inch lengths
1/4 cup diced tomatoes
1 ounce grated havarti cheese; about 1/2 cup lightly packed

Follow the above directions, substituting asparagus for mushrooms. Remove the pan from the heat and add the tomatoes to the asparagus. Follow the directions for omelet (left).

Bacon, Onion, Red Bell Pepper and Spicy Monterey Jack
Makes 1 omelet

1 strip bacon, diced
1/4 cup minced onion; about 1/2 small onion
1/4 cup diced red bell pepper; less than 1/2 a red bell pepper
1 ounce grated Pepper Jack cheese; about 1/2 cup lightly packed

Following the above directions, add the bacon to the pan without butter. When the bacon is done, remove it with a slotted spoon and drain it on a paper towel. Remove all but 1/2 tablespoon of bacon fat and add the onions and peppers to the pan. Sauté until tender, about 5 to 7 minutes and set aside in a small bowl. Follow the directions for omelet (left).

Almost anything can go into an omelet - leftover cheeses, meats, lobster, Pesto Roasted Aspragus, Broccoli with Roasted Red Onion, Kale Salad, Melty Cheese and Spinach Appetizers ... and on and on. Eggs are a versatile blank slate on which to paint your creative dinner.

December

The sun goes down so early this time of year that by 4:30 P.M. it's completely dark. By 5 P.M. we feel as if we should be having dinner; and by 6 P.M. it feels as if it's bed time! The holidays arrive at the perfect time to bring light to our winter hibernation, with candles for the advent wreath and lights on the Christmas tree. We all lay under the tree, looking up at the lights from below, telling tales and sometimes reading our favorite Christmas stories to each other.

Basic Waffle Recipe

Makes 10 to 12 waffles

2 cups all-purpose flour
1/4 cup sugar
1 1/2 teaspoons baking powder
1 teaspoon baking soda
1 teaspoon salt
3 eggs, separated
1/2 cup (1 stick) unsalted butter, melted
1 3/4 cups buttermilk

Preheat the waffle iron. In a large mixing bowl, sift all dry ingredients. Mix the egg yolks, butter, and buttermilk in a medium bowl. Combine with the dry ingredients. In a separate bowl – one that is clean and dry – beat the egg whites until they form stiff peaks. Fold into the batter, then follow the directions for your waffle iron.

Lemon Poppy Seed Waffles

These, if pressed, would have to be my families' favorite, but it's a hard choice to make and one where Lemon Poppy seed doesn't always come out on top. We especially like these with fresh strawberries sprinkled with demerara or turbinado sugar for crunch.

To the Basic Waffle recipe
Add: 2 tablespoons poppy seeds
2 teaspoons lemon zest; about 1 lemon
6 tablespoons lemon juice; about 1 lemon
2 teaspoons lemon extract

Add poppy seeds when you're combining the dry ingredients. Add the zest, lemon juice, and lemon extract when you're mixing the egg yolks, butter, and buttermilk.

Coconut, Orange, and Chocolate Waffles

Served with orange segments (supreme) sprinkled with demerera sugar and toasted coconut on top if you like. Maple syrup is maybe an afterthought here rather than the main event.

To the Basic Waffle recipe
Substitute: 1/4 cup lightly packed brown sugar for 1/4 cup sugar
Add: 2 tablespoons buttermilk

2 teaspoons coconut extract
2 teaspoons orange extract
2 teaspoons orange zest
1/2 cup toasted coconut
3/4 cup chopped semi-sweet chocolate (or chips)

Add the extra buttermilk, extracts and zest when you're mixing the egg yolks, butter, and buttermilk. Follow the instructions as listed in the Basic Waffle recipe. Add the coconut and chocolate at the end.

Potato Cilantro Waffles

This recipe is a perfect way to use up leftover mashed potatoes. If the potatoes are cold from the refrigerator, warm them up a little bit in the microwave, and then add in some of the buttermilk slowly, with a potato masher, so you work most of the clumps out. Dill is a perfect substitute for cilantro in this recipe.

Soft-boiled or poached eggs are a perfect match for these waffles. When asparagus is in season, we like to steam it, adding a little sea salt and lemon juice at the end and then layer it with waffles and the eggs making a meal that's just as good for dinner as it is for breakfast.

To the Basic Waffle recipe
Add: 3/4 pound Yukon Gold potatoes; about 1 medium potato
(or 1 cup leftover mashed potatoes)
2 tablespoons minced fresh cilantro

Peel the potato and cut into large pieces. Boil in salted water over high heat until tender. Remove from heat and drain. Mash the potatoes and cilantro together with a potato masher. Set aside to cool. Combine the buttermilk and potatoes together first. Follow the instructions as listed in the Basic Waffle recipe.

Rum Raisin Vanilla Waffles

Reserve the scraped vanilla bean and place in a jar of sugar to make vanilla sugar for another recipe.

To the Basic Waffle recipe
Add: 1 cup raisins
1/2 cup Goslings rum or other dark rum
1 vanilla bean, split lengthwise and seeds scraped
Substitute: 1/4 cup lightly packed brown sugar for 1/4 cup sugar
Reduce: buttermilk to 1 1/2 cups buttermilk

Soak the raisins in the rum for 20 minutes to 1 hour. Whisk the scraped seeds from the vanilla bean and the brown sugar into the buttermilk, then whisk in the egg yolks. Add the raisins and rum and then follow the instructions as listed in the Basic Waffle recipe.

Chipotle Chocolate Waffles

Chipotle en adobo can be found in the Mexican specialty section of most grocery stores or a Mexican grocery. One tablespoon makes this just spicy enough for half of my family to notice and enjoy it. The other half prefers less, so gauge your crowd.

Queso fresco or Mexican crèma are both lovely with these waffles as is sour cream. The heat is balanced well by the softness of the chocolate, but if you don't care for spicy food, feel free to bump the amount of chipotle down.

To the Basic Waffle recipe
Substitute: 1/4 cup lightly packed brown sugar for 1/4 cup sugar
Add: 1 tablespoon minced chipotle en adobo
3/4 cup bittersweet chocolate, coarsely chopped

Whisk the chipotle en adobe and brown sugar into the buttermilk to make sure it gets broken up and incorporated; then whisk in the egg yolks. Follow the instructions as listed in the Basic Waffle recipe. Add the chocolate at the end.

Mocha Waffles

By themselves, these waffles wish for a little more sugar; but once you add maple syrup into the equation, a heavenly balance is struck.

To the Basic Waffle recipe
Substitute: 1/4 cup lightly packed brown sugar for 1/4 cup sugar
Reduce: flour to 1 3/4 cups all-purpose flour
Add: 1/4 cup Dutch process cocoa powder
2 teaspoons instant coffee granules
1 vanilla bean, split lengthwise and seeds scraped

Add the cocoa powder to the dry ingredients. In a medium bowl, whisk together the egg yolks, butter, buttermilk, brown sugar, coffee and vanilla seeds. Follow the instructions as listed in the Basic Waffle recipe.

BY HAND
Felted Trivets

Functional and beautiful. Useful and lovely. Efficient and charming. It's the marriage of these two – the practical and the whimsical that I'm drawn to every time. I like art for art's sake. I do. But what really gets me going, what really brings moments of joy to my day are things that I use every single day that are not just useful but are delightful to my senses. Like the tea cozy I made years ago from scrap upholstery fabric and an old wool sweater. I use it every morning to keep our pot of coffee hot, and nearly every day get a little extra spot of happiness from using such a familiar friend. (I suppose I should call it a coffee cozy now because it's only on the rare winter afternoon that it's used for tea.)

Hand-felted wool trivets are another kitchen tool that I use every day; and each time I use them, for a moment, just a second, I think to myself, 'This trivet makes me happy.' I blink, the moment is gone, and I'm off to something else; but that wisp of 'happy' lingers.

Simple moments like these are treasures akin to walking down the street, holding hands with my daughters; or taking a quiet moment on a lobster bake to appreciate the beauty of Penobscot Bay. It's just a blink and then it's gone, but one to notice, pay attention to and savor. For me, this is a life well lived – wending from one tiny cheerful moment to the next.

To make a trivet, you can purchase carded wool at any fiber arts store. I still have raw wool from an entire garbage bag purchased one year at the Common Ground Fair (our local fair run by Maine Organic Farmers and Gardeners Association), so this is typically what I use for my felting projects. The girls and I bought a set of carding paddles at the same time and when they were small would sit together carding wool while listening to a story on tape as a quiet afternoon activity. The girls loved it because it was something they could do and feel accomplished at as they watched their pile of fluffy wool grow with each pass.

We also felt on the *Riggin* in the afternoon, again for something to do that is quiet and together. It becomes a little like a quilting circle where crew and guests join to learn or just chat. Sometimes we'll make colorful wool beads that become buttons for clothes; other

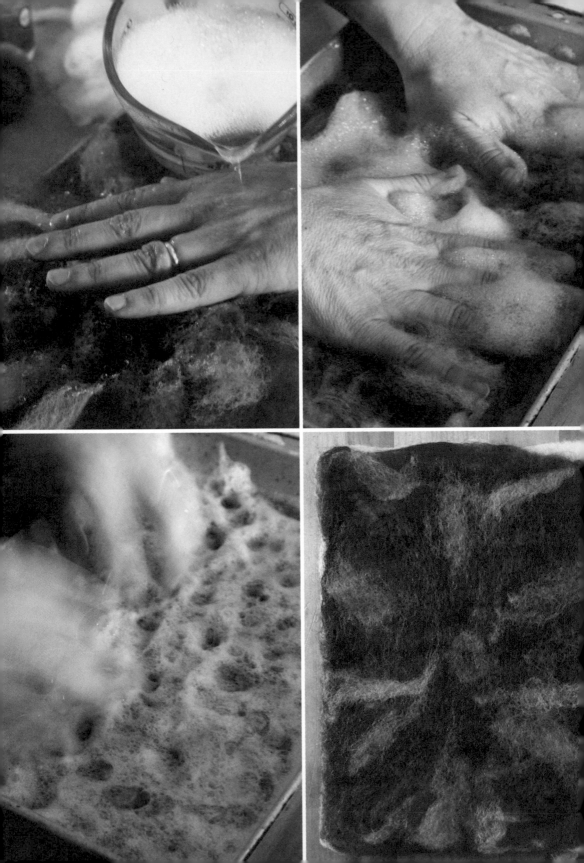

times a felted purse or slippers. In any case, as I look back on all of our projects, I'm not surprised to note that they all serve a function and are beautiful as well.

Felted Trivet

Materials
Un-dyed carded wool in a neutral color of your choice
Dyed carded wool in several colors of your choice
Liquid dish soap, preferably biodegradable; about 1/2 teaspoon to 1 cup water
Water — both really warm and cold

1. Choose a kitchen pan that is the size of the trivet you would like to create.

2. Lay the neutral colored wool in even, crisscrossing (perpendicular) layers in the bottom of the pan to about 3-inches thick.

3. Arrange the colored wool, in any pattern you would like, as the top layer. This layer is decorative and does not need to be thick.

4. Gently add warm soapy water, being careful to not disturb the decorative wool. The piece should be distinctly wet, but not floating.

5. Ever so gently begin to massage the wool with either your finger tips or your flat hands. I begin by just pressing my hands onto the wool and increase the agitation slowly.

6. As the fibers begin to come together you can begin to work the piece a little more assertively; turn the piece over and working the back side as well. This can take around 15 minutes.

7. As the water cools, drain it and add either really warm water or cold water. When you alternate, the difference in temperature helps to get the fibers to lock onto each other.

8. When the piece feels solid and firm, rinse well in cold water. If there are any flaps of felt (my family calls them "nibbles" but this is not a technical term) use a pair of scissors to snip them off.

9. Roll the trivet in a towel and press out the water and set in a warm place to dry.

Acknowledgements

Writing seems to be such a solo process that we tend to think that books are written by one person and one person alone. The writer is, after all, the author and their name is on the cover. In reality, while no one else types the keys of the keyboard for me, nor thinks my thoughts, this book was a fun, interesting, collaborative process. There were more than a few essential people who helped me organize these thoughts into what you are able to easily and coherently read and see. My work is made better by those individuals, to whom I am deeply grateful, for both their collaboration, and their generous spirits.

To E, for every day made even better by working and laughing our way through each decision, email and pile of paper. And for your photos, without which my food could not be seen.

To Maria, Christopher and Ryan from MORE and Co., for their creativity, inspiration, collaboration and visual clarity. This book was made ever so much MORE by your dynamic trio!

To Dana, for knowing me, and my writing, and making it even better, cleaner, funnier, smarter and more organized. With you one plus one makes more than two.

To Dave Osterman and Norma Mahle, bless you for your sharp eye for detail and your willingness to look at anything I sent you.

To ALL of the recipe testers whether on the *Riggin*, in my home, or in your own homes; your feedback is invaluable. My team in no particular order because those with last names beginning with 'Z' get the short end of the stick sometimes! - Nancy Knott, Joan Guarino, Charles Depew, Ann Pare, Jane Peak, Cindy Holden, Al Thibodeau, Tish Gallagher, Patricia Johns, Pinky Rines, Jim Perley, Jeff Campbell, Cindy Frederick, Susan McBean, Karin Wren, Karen Courington, Patricia Wisneski, Rose Chillemi, Julie Thiessen, Karen Cronin, Joyce Riddle, Dotty Craig, Will & Donna Farmer, Susan Land, Diane Goeser, Terry Danner and Diane Agostino.

To all of the farmers, growers and producers who have a place at my table whether through their food or their actual presence, what I create every day would pale without your attention to detail and your care of the products you grow, raise and create.

To Rebecca Jacobs for all that goes into and comes out of our beautiful gardens, thank you.

To Sharon Kitchens, for always believing that ours is a good story — and sharing that story with others.

To Jon, the man who holds my hand while we walk through life together. After 23 years my heart is STILL big for you.

To our children, who are of us, but not owned by us. The universe and your Papa and I are so blessed to have you in our lives.